HAUNTED
IOWA CITY

HAUNTED IOWA CITY

VERNON TROLLINGER

Haunted America

Published by Haunted America
A Division of The History Press
Charleston, SC 29403
www.historypress.net

Unless otherwise noted, all images are by the author.

First published 2011

Manufactured in the United States

ISBN 978.1.60949.286.1

Library of Congress CIP data applied for.

Notice: The information in this book is true and complete to the best of our knowledge. It is offered without guarantee on the part of the author or The History Press. The author and The History Press disclaim all liability in connection with the use of this book.

CONTENTS

ACKNOWLEDGEMENTS

Thanks to the following people who took a little bit of their time to provide me with huge details and helpful information while collecting the history and legends of haunted Iowa City:

Denise K. Anderson and the staff at University Archives.
Ray and Shirley Hendrickson at the beautiful Mission House Bed and
    Breakfast.
Pastor Robert Dotzel at Christas House and Brett Gordon at Old Brick.
Don Flack and Kristi Nielson.
Marlin Ingalls at the Iowa Office of the State Archaeologist.
Kirk Stephan, founder of the Hall Mall.
Bob Hibbs for both the Schneider Building and Mary Herrick timelines.
George Volk for the stories and great tour into the bowels of City High.
Timothy C. Parrot, whose booklet, *The Enigma of Theresa Dolezal Feldwert*, is
    required reading for any student of the Black Angel and Czech settlement
    in Goose Town.
And especially the *Third Eye Over Iowa* staff writers. Believe at Your Own Risk.

THE UN-HAUNTING OF
109 EAST MARKET STREET

Usually while investigating a house reported to be haunted, you learn about how humans behave and how they interpret their environment. You also learn just how far afield interpretation likes to wander. Take, for example, the case of 109 East Market Street.

The house is one of the oldest brick houses in Iowa City, dating from between 1850 and 1860. Its exterior architectural style is a mixture of Greek Revival, Second Empire and Picturesque. These styles traveled slowly from Europe to the U.S. East Coast and then across the Midwest. The porch sports a Doric temple façade entrance with paired wooden columns that greet the visitor with formality but nearly engulf one near the door. The front hallway is narrow and high ceilinged. To the left is a formal meeting room, though originally it may have been a parlor. To the right is what can be called a modern living room, though it may have once been a sitting room or study. This room is in the newer section of the building, thought to have been added between 1860 and 1870. A wooden addition for the kitchen was added possibly in the 1870s as well.

The house had been owned for several years by Gloria Dei Lutheran Church, which operated it as a rental property until it was converted in 2006 into Christus House, a student center for the Lutheran Campus Ministry at the University of Iowa. It is currently supervised by Pastor Robert Dotzel. During conversation at church one day, the topic of my research into ghost stories in Iowa City came up, and Pastor Rob invited me to come next door to Christus House to talk to the two students living there.

109 East Market Street, Christas House. Weird mummified bat altar or just old Halloween party decorations?

Roger was a dark-haired, gangly kid in his early twenties. We met briefly in the living room, but he was rushing off for an appointment. He told me that he had heard strange noises in his room since he had moved in, including footsteps in the dead of night that began at his front window and moved east toward the wall—and kept going beyond.

I made a note of it and then stopped into Pastor Rob's office. We talked a bit about the noises and the architecture and history of the house. Then, he said he wanted to tell me a story about the basement. As we went down the steep, short stairway into the cramped, ancient basement, he took me to a section bordered by a massive, foreboding brick wall with wide, sloping footings that were two to three feet thick. They reminded me of the brick walls in Poe's "Cask of Amontillado." As it turned out, this wall supported the center wall of the house (which had originally been the exterior west wall). "This was the spot," Rob said. "Here's where we found the dead bat with the candles."

When I heard that, I think Rob actually heard my brain's main drive sprocket snap off a tooth. He smiled and began telling me the story:

When we first moved the campus ministry in here after the students left, we cleaned the place out. Down here, we found a desiccated dead bat hanging by its leg just above the floor. It was surrounded by a ring of candles, and there were also candles arranged on the brick wall. [He pointed to the top ledge of the wall's massive footing.] *I'm no expert, but it looked like some kind of altar, and with those students that lived here—I mean, you just don't know what they were doing. This place was wet and dirty, and there were critters back under the crawl spaces. Anyway, one of the things we did was conduct a whole house blessing. I went through each floor and said a prayer. When we got here, I spent a little extra time because—well, I just don't like to think about what may have been going on.*

Intrigued, I came back later that week and talked at length with Roger and Ben, the other student living in the house. I mentioned the bat in the cellar, and Roger confessed that the idea spooked him. The house made noises at night, and he was concerned that they were not alone. Ben, meanwhile, didn't believe any of it. He had been working on repairing damage made by all the critters that had burrowed or nested in the attic or crept in through broken basement windows. Some of these included squirrels getting up under the eaves and bats that hid in crawl spaces under the kitchen floor.

Before I left for the day, Pastor Rob gave me a copy of a student research paper he had found when they first moved in. It was by Marie Gernes for a class called Place Studies and was dated 2005. It outlined the history of the building and its architecture and gave an interpretation of how its meaning as a structure had changed from *home* to *house* over time.

The original lot is referred to on period maps as the "Sanxay Homestead" and was purchased by Frederic Sanxay in 1842. Sanxay was a banker who operated a mercantile business in Iowa City beginning in 1840 at Clinton Street and Iowa Avenue. The family later built the Whetstone building on Washington and Clinton Streets, which housed a drugstore and soda fountain for many years and is now Panchero's Mexican restaurant. In 1920, the Plant family bought the home. In 1946, the Gilmore family bought the house after Dr. Gilmore retired as president of the University of Iowa. In 1967, Mrs. Gilmore told Professor Margaret Keyes (author of *Nineteenth Century Architecture in Iowa City*) that the foundation stones were left over from the building of the Old Capitol. In 1976, the home was subdivided into smaller apartments by the Gilmore children. It was sold a few years later to the next-door neighbor, Gloria Dei Lutheran Church.

Using the paper as a historical guide, I delved into researching some of the darker practices of some pagan cults or would-be witches. I found myself wondering if something truly weird was going on. Had occult forces that had once lain dormant in the house been lured forth by the grotesque bat rite? Were these same forces only just kept in check by Pastor Rob's blessing? I scoured through newspaper archives looking for instances of violent crime that might have occurred in the past. All in all, it was a complete wash. I found nothing—not even the slightest indication that Dr. Gilmore himself ever uttered the Lord's name in vain, scolded a squirrel or even upbraided a bat.

The next step was to contact Marie Gernes. I found her still living in town and working on her doctoral degree. When I asked her about the bat, things rapidly fell into place.

Gernes and her housemates had moved into the first floor in 2004. They immediately fell in love with the house's creepy basement, where they discovered a mummified bat hanging by its leg from a string. That was all the motivation they needed to throw a Halloween party, complete with decorations and candles arranged around the little dried-out carcass. But like any house full of college students, none of them felt very much like cleaning up the next day after the party. So the candles and the disgusting dried-out bat languished—first for weeks, then months and then, two years later, it was time for them to move out.

The bat, meanwhile, had probably been caught by a former tenant. According to Ben, who had been busy repairing several basement windows, he had found guano showing where bats had been living in the crawl space beneath the kitchen. A few years earlier, then, it was possible that a bat had made its way through the crawl space and in through one of the old broken windows in the basement. Very probably, a former tenant trapped it somehow and tied a string to its leg for amusement. Yes, just like playing with a rubber bat on a string—only it was real. College students will entertain themselves with just about anything.

Pastor Rob laughed heartily at my detective work, partly from surprise but also from relief. Human neglect and lassitude are simple, normal behaviors compared to occult rituals for mummified bats. In that context, Pastor Rob found them very comforting versus the dark, demonic rites he had undoubtedly been imagining.

The story of 109 East Market Street is an example of most old houses in Iowa City. With students and scholars coming and going every year, old houses accrete jumbled clues about the previous residents at a higher-than-normal rate. Each year, when new people come to town, they try to make sense of their surroundings. They misread the clues and fabricate stories about these places. Not surprisingly, the stories about many of these places are way more fantastic—and often way more believed—than the factual history.

THE HALL MALL

If you stroll along the Ped Mall on College Street, you might chance to see a simple black-and-white arrow sign pointing up with the name "Hall Mall" written on it. Next to it is a glass door and, beyond that, a steep stairway leading up to 114½ East College Street. Starting in 1970 and through the 1990s, that door led to a weird but magical place that belied the staid Jackson's Gifts and China store below it.

If you were a student at the time, you entered the most unique and grooviest place west of the Mississippi and east of the Iowa. When you opened that door, you were enveloped in a fog of patchouli incense and the cacophony of two or three musical styles. At the top of the stairs, the first thing you came to was the long corridor with a very high tin ceiling. The worn linoleum floor heaved up slightly in the middle. A bench that wrapped all the way around one of the support posts beckoned two-thirds down the hallway. On either side, there were stern-looking office doors with transom windows dating from the late 1920s or 1930s. It looked for all the world like Sam Spade should stride out from one of these doors, hang a cigarette in his lips and ask you for a light.

But instead, here was the coolest assortment of little shops selling funky secondhand clothing, handmade jewelry, used records, used CDs, used books, alternative magazines, guitars, waterbed sheets and bulbous-shaped, water-filled smoking apparatuses. At one point, there was even a small zoo, with snakes and monkeys and more, until the city's animal control department removed the animals when the owner abandoned it.

The Schneider Building, 114 East College Street. The door and stairs up to the Hall Mall are on the lower right.

Many of the shopkeepers put in long days in their stores and worked late into the night. Some, like the Hall Mall's founder, Kirk Stephan, even lived there (paying only thirty dollars a month for rent). Over the years, lots of people came through the Hall Mall, with almost as many shops opening and then moving on. The place was filled with lots of stories, some scarcely recalled. But one that lingers to this day is that people who are alone and working late in the Hall Mall hear footsteps just outside their door walking down the corridor. When these shopkeepers look up and down the hall, there's nobody there.

The stories of the mysterious footsteps have long been woven into the Hall Mall's character. In the 1980s and 1990s, it seemed that everyone knew a friend of a friend who had heard them. Someone invented the notion that the footsteps belonged to "George." The nickname stuck for a number of years but seems to have since faded.

Some who don't know the Hall Mall might explain that a shopkeeper would need to walk from the back of his store to the door to look out into the hallway. By that time, the person making the noise would be gone. However, Hall Mall stores are small, only eight feet by twelve feet. To block shoplifting and to allow space for their wares, most store owners set up their purchase and workspaces next to their doors. All they have to do is tilt their heads into the doorway to see the entire hallway.

Sure, the Hall Mall is in an old brick building. Originally under construction at 114 and 116 East College Street as the G.W. Marquardt building in 1881, it was later bought by the Schneider Brothers sometime after 1892 and is still known as the Schneider Building. Old brick buildings shift and move, though not as readily as wood-framed buildings. Most of the movement happens during bitterly cold winter nights, causing the whole structure to contract, making the beams groan, pop and squeak. Kirk Stephan shrugs off the footstep stories as noise from the alley behind the building resonating in the garbage chute at the end of the hall.

But footsteps *walking past a door*?

And there are also those strange shadows at the far end of the hall. In those cases, witnesses report hearing footsteps late at night in the hall. When they look out their doorways, they don't see anyone but notice a faint shadow shifting in front of the covered-up window at the end of the hall until it fades.

But what incidents and activities cause these phenomena to materialize in a place that long ago sold furniture? What is so compellingly paranormal about a place that sold dressers, tables and armoires?

The Hall Mall. Shifting shadows sometimes seen at the far end in front of the old windows are rumored to be those of George the ghost.

Today, the answer is surprising. Only a century ago, it was common for cabinetmakers to make furnishings for both the living and the dead.

In 1892, the Schneider Brothers (Alois, Frank, Henry, John and William) were in the furniture business at 210 Washington Street. As was common for cabinetmakers, they also built coffins—which is really just a different type of cabinet. Consequently, it seemed a natural leap for the business to fully diversify into such an important local service sector slot. Alois, Henry and William trained as morticians. Schneider Brothers then took up undertaking, including storing dead bodies and preparing them for burial. Competition in Iowa City among undertakers was pretty lively at the time. In the immediate downtown area, there were four or five funeral parlors in buildings that now house bookstores, restaurants or bars. Both the furniture and undertaking businesses for the brothers went well, and sometime after 1892, they bought the spacious building at 114–116 East College Street and set up shop. By 1904, they had acquired 118 East College and moved their mortuary business there. A closed doorway at the top of the Hall Mall stairs on the right leads into this building, but it is usually locked. Until the spring of 2011, it was a bar known as Vito's.

Sometime in the early 1920s, however, the Schneider Brothers left the furniture business. The main floor of 114–116 East College was leased to White's Consolidated Stores, a department store chain. The upper floors were subdivided into small office spaces for lawyers, bond dealers and insurance agents. The small, cramped spaces seen today are very much the same as they were then. Next door at 118 East College, the upper floor was also subdivided for similar business renters, while the main floor remained a funeral parlor. The Schneider Brothers moved their business to 230 South Dubuque Street sometime before 1930. (An exact date isn't readily available. An obituary in the *Iowa City Press-Citizen* for 1928 reads, "The body is now at Schneider Brothers funeral parlor, where it may be viewed by friends up until the hour of the funeral." However, neither the old nor new address was printed.)

The Schneider Building, meanwhile, attracted a series of new ventures. After White's Consolidated Stores, it became a Scott Department Store (subsidiary of Butler Brothers of Chicago) in the 1930s and a Kinney's shoes in the 1960s through 1973. In 1970, Kirk Stephan rented an office space upstairs to open his own small jewelry shop, Emerald City, and the Hall Mall was born.

The early twenty-first century, though, has been hard on the Hall Mall. The Internet now provides young entrepreneurs with even cheaper virtual storefronts versus what this old building offers. Yet while there are fewer stores here, several bands use the spaces for rehearsals and performances.

During those thirty or so years on College Street, Schneider Brothers served families from all kinds of backgrounds. In the First World War, they prepared the bodies of Iowa City's soldiers who fell in battle and were returned home. They helped bury the town's dead from the Spanish flu epidemic in 1918. They embalmed the wealthy stockbroker and the hardworking farmer. One wonders, though, if the footsteps and vague shadows belong to any of these folks. One report from the 1990s hints at more than just a returning customer.

In the 1990s, a small book and magazine store named Moon Mystique set up in the front room of the Hall Mall. It carried a wide variety of local magazines but primarily catered to piercing and pagan spiritualists. Late one night, a young man working at Moon Mystique was dismayed by the torrential downpour outside. Movement caught his eye, and he turned to see a farmer walk past the door dressed in bib overalls and a seed hat. The worker went back to taking inventory until it struck him that the farmer was bone dry and wasn't making a sound on the creaky floor outside the store. He went out into the hall and saw the apparition dissolve into thin air.

While the story describes the old man as a farmer, it is just as likely that the old man may have been a cabinetmaker, because a century ago, such a craftsman would have worn overalls, too. If that is the case, maybe one of the Schneider Brothers or a dedicated employee—perhaps even named George—is still working late just like all those shopkeepers who have seen or heard him.

GRAVE MISDEEDS

THE WANDERING CADAVER

The black crepe ribbon on the front door of 1310 Cedar Street shook in the harsh wind that gray December 29 in 1870. Mrs. Mary Herrick, age seventy, had died late on the night of December 27. Widowed since 1841, Mary left an adult son named Charles Henry, an adult daughter named Frances and seven grandchildren.

Amid the grief of loss, her son-in-law's house had been bustling with the proper activities of mourning as befitting a family of Mrs. Herrick's social station. Her daughter, Frances Kimball, dutifully went through the house stopping clocks, putting sheets over mirrors and making certain all photos had been placed facedown so that her mother's spirit would not hide in the mirrors or seek to possess the living. Family and friends were alerted of the death. Frances sent her son, Charles, into town to tell her brother, his uncle and namesake, and also had him visit their close friends, the Irish family. Frances and her husband, Dr. George Kimball (a retired physician and well-known horticulturist), then summoned one of the better undertakers from downtown to arrange for the burial in the new family plot in Oakland Cemetery.

The sexton and his assistant at Oakland Cemetery took the news of digging a winter grave with a sigh of resignation. They knew well that death had no season, but digging a grave in Iowa during the winter was

1310 Cedar Street, once owned by Dr. and Mrs. George Kimball and the site of Mary Herrick's funeral in December 1870. A retired physician turned horticulturist, Dr. Kimball enjoyed betting on horse races. His gambling may have lost his family's home in 1879.

never welcomed work, no matter what the pay. Still, they fell to chunking through the granite-like frozen earth with pick and shovel. The job took them the better part of the day, and upon finishing, they covered the dirt pile with a tarp to keep it from freezing back into a solid block. With professional aplomb, they kicked away loose dirt clods from the graveside, picked up their spent liquor bottles and then withdrew a few discreet paces away to wait by a small fire.

At the appointed afternoon hour, the front door of the house on Cedar Street opened, and the pallbearers carrying Mrs. Herrick's coffin emerged. One of these was John P. Irish, editor of the *Iowa Daily Press* newspaper, former statehouse member, state Democratic Party chairman and trustee of the University of Iowa. Little did John Irish know just how heavily the fate of Mrs. Herrick's corpse would weigh upon his own.

John Irish was the third son of one of Iowa City's founders, Frederick Macy Irish. His older brother Gilbert was a noted horticulturist and historian who shared his interests with Dr. George Kimball and helped train Kimball's son, the younger Charles. Irish's other older brother, Charles Wood, was a civil and mining engineer who knew Charles Henry Herrick, himself a civil and mining engineer.

John Irish, meanwhile, had struck out in a more public direction than his brothers. In addition to his journalistic and political endeavors, his most recent accomplishment was helping establish the new Medical College at the University of Iowa. Though only offering classes for thirty-seven students since autumn of 1870, the idea of founding a medical college in Iowa City had been a political lightning rod since the end of the Civil War. Its chief rival lay coiled in the southern corner of the state at Keokuk, where a medical college had been set up by wealthy doctors and ambitious politicians. The competition for talent, regulating authority and the money that would follow was often rancorous and vitriolic—especially because none of the Keokuk faculty was invited to join the new institution in Iowa City. Consequently, opponents of the Iowa City school watched and waited for any excuse to close its doors.

Two days after Mary Herrick's funeral, on Saturday morning, December 31, the sky still bore its sepulchral gray as the sexton came to the end of his morning rounds. He had just turned back for the warmth of the squat office shack when the sight of loose earth littering the ground a few yards away caught his eye and stopped him with alarm. As he drew near the spot, what should have been a neat, low mound over the fresh grave was a sloppy, uneven pile of dirt.

That afternoon, a member of the city council joined members of the cemetery board to investigate. The sexton turned over a notebook he had found lying next to the grave. The name on the front read "D. Bradley." The men exchanged concerned frowns. Dominick Bradley was a reputed ruffian who worked for the brand-new Medical College. In only a few minutes, the sexton and his assistant had shoveled down to the coffin lid. They opened it. Mary Herrick's body was gone.

A little past 4:00 p.m., Dr. Kimball and his son Charles burst into Charles Henry Herrick's office, slamming the door behind them. "I have grim news," Kimball said, holding up his hand to keep his brother-in-law in his chair.

"It must be very grave to bring both of you here," Herrick observed.

"Grave is precisely the term, my dear fellow," the old doctor muttered, barely able to control his emotions. "Your mother's grave, in fact."

Herrick stared back blankly, shocked.

"Grandma's body has been taken, uncle," the younger Charles explained. "Mother and father believe it now lies in the Medical College at South Hall."

Without another word, the three set out onto the already darkening streets. Shortly thereafter, they had climbed the steps of South Hall on the University of Iowa campus, just a few yards south of the Old State Capitol, and began shouting and pounding its oaken doors, each barely controlling his frustration and rage. Its doors locked, they hoped one of the body-snatching scoundrels inside would have the temerity to confront them. But no answer came, and the men noted that neither sparks nor white wisps of smoke swirled from the building's chimneys. The trio split up, racing around the building looking for a way in, until the old doctor shouted for his fellows to join him at the back. There in the gathering gloom, the three spied a faint glow of gaslight coming from inside.

Herrick spoke in a low, quavering voice. "What are they doing with her?"

"Hopefully nothing more than taking measurements. But we must get the sheriff to investigate this building before further desecrations are committed," the doctor replied.

With that, they hurried just a few blocks away to the county attorney's office at the Johnson County Courthouse. After hearing their story, the prosecutor agreed to secure a warrant to search the building. Because it was Saturday night and New Year's Eve, the wheels of justice dawdled. It took five hours until the signed warrant was delivered to the sheriff.

Meanwhile, news about the cemetery outrage flowed like nickel beer at a ballpark. As the saloons filled up in anticipation of New Year's toasts, anger seethed with the news that the sheriff had decided not to execute the search warrant until the morning. Anger so touched the crowd that they resolved to organize a guard around South Hall to prevent anyone from coming or leaving unnoticed—right after they finished their beers.

It was ten minutes to midnight when a sharp rapping on his office door woke John Irish. Irish looked at the clock on the wall from where he had fallen asleep at his desk. He opened the door. There stood the hotel clerk. "There are two gents to see you at the back door," the clerk said.

Irish shook his senses back into order and made his way down the stairs, past the front desk and out the back door to the alley entrance.

"Mr. Irish, sir," a young man said as he stepped out from the shadow.

"Yes, what do you want?" Irish asked impatiently. He sized up the youth in front of him and noted the other one standing a short distance away, furtively looking up and down the alley.

"You have no doubt heard that a grave was robbed, sir."

"Oh no," he moaned and put his hand to his face.

"Please, sir. We need your help," the young man pleaded.

John P. Irish (1843–1923), editor of the *Iowa State Press*, a member of the Twelfth, Thirteenth and Fourteenth General Assemblies of Iowa and trustee of the University of Iowa.

As the self-appointed guards arrived to take up positions around the building, they failed to notice that from the back of South Hall, two figures hurried through the thickets down the bluff toward the river. They bore an awkward burden with them bundled in a blanket or sheet, but it was difficult to be sure, for as they neared the riverbank, the pair vanished in the chill midnight mist.

The sheriff got an early start on business that New Year's Day. He had already searched Dr. Boucher's residence and found nothing. Next, he and his deputies commenced with searching South Hall. In the basement, they discovered one medical student painstakingly studying a dilapidated, alcohol-bloated male specimen that the student called "Moses." But of Mrs. Herrick, there was neither hide nor hair to be found.

A few minutes before noon, Dr. Kimball and Charles Henry Herrick entered John Irish's office at the Clinton House Hotel. They apologized for being late, but both had come directly from meeting with the sheriff at South Hall and were grumbling about the miserable delay by both the judge and the sheriff in searching the place.

Irish listened sympathetically until they finished their story. Then, he leaned forward in his chair and spoke with soft urgency. "We can waste no more time in this. Let me propose a solution. I will send letters to those in the Medical College urging those ghouls who took your mother's remains to return them anonymously by placing them in a coffin that we will station in an alley behind the undertakers in the block opposite. Now, in order for this to occur, I ask that you promise to let the matter drop entirely once you have recovered the body."

"You think this will work?" asked Herrick.

"I think these devils have very few options left," Irish answered. "They know that sooner or later they will be caught and their medical futures irreparably damaged."

"What time do you plan for this?" asked Dr. Kimball.

"Tonight, between 11:30 and 12:30. This will give them a wide opportunity to make sure they are not being watched and see that we are playing fairly. I'm sure they will leave the remains," Irish explained.

The brothers-in-law looked at each other and nodded in agreement.

The clock in the dimly lit front parlor of the undertaker's shop clacked off the seconds as Irish, Herrick and Dr. Kimball waited for news from the back of the shop. Finally, at 11:45 p.m., the mortician emerged from the shadows in the back, announcing, "She has been returned."

As Herrick and the doctor rose from their seats, the mortician took a step toward them and said, "There is a problem."

Irish stared in shock at the man and then at the brothers-in-law. Both men glared, Herrick's jaw malevolently set. In an instant, Herrick bolted past the mortician with Dr. Kimball behind. Irish trotted a few steps behind the two as they wound through the back room and out into the alley.

The coffin lay closed on the ground. A glowing lantern sat on the ground beside it. Herrick snatched up the lantern and threw open the casket just as

Dr. Kimball and Irish crowded next to him. A figure draped in a filthy sheet lay inside. Pieces of straw stuck out from the covering at odd angles. There was also the unmistakable stink of formaldehyde. Dr. Kimball squatted down and drew aside the flap covering the face.

Herrick recoiled, letting out a loud groan of horror and anger. Inside the casket lay his dear mother, her face barely recognizable. One side had been mostly defleshed, revealing the delicate web of nerves, veins and arteries weaving across the exposed teeth, cheek and jawbones that glowed yellow-white in the lantern light. Her naked eye stared crazily up at them from its boney orbit.

"Savages!" Dr. Kimball spat in anger, hastily recovering the face.

"Monstrous," Irish gasped. Suddenly, Herrick grabbed him by the lapels of his coat and threw him hard against the nearby wall.

"This is your doing! That medical college of yours is a den of goddamned butchers!" Herrick shouted, and then he cuffed Irish smartly across the cheek hard enough to make the newsman stumble.

Dr. Kimball pulled Herrick inside before any more damage could be done. A moment later, the mortician and his assistant came out into the alley. They reclosed the casket and carried it inside. Irish, sensing he had worn out his welcome, walked out onto the street and made his way back to his office.

The next morning, the Herrick family vented their rage in the *Iowa City Republican Citizen*. Their public letter revealed the details of the partial dissection of their mother and announced that the deal with the grave robbers was off. They declared that if the city's citizens wanted to be sure that their departed relatives would rest undisturbed, they had "better annihilate the medical department and raze the building to the ground."

Telegraphs chattered the story across the state. Outrage and disgust exploded in newspapers all over the state at the nefarious deed done by "medical hyenas attending the University." In very short order, the perpetrators were rounded up: the janitor, Dominique Bradley, confessed, and warrants for grave robbing were issued for the two medical students who helped him, as well as Dr. Boucher and John P. Irish.

Irish faced not only the disappointment of his own family but also the bitterness of the Herrick clan. Doubtless, too, he sensed what surely must have seemed death's own hand upon his political career.

Even though Dominick Bradley turned state's evidence, the grand jury elected not to charge anyone. All five men were set free within one month. Under pressure, Dr. Boucher promptly resigned and moved

Oakland Cemetery's old tombstone inscriptions are weathered away, and some graves are no longer marked. Mary Herrick, where are you?

to California, but not before recommending to the governor that the unclaimed bodies of prisoners who died in state penitentiaries should be used for anatomical instruction. The legislature quickly enacted the policy into law. Some wag may have wished Dr. Boucher "God's speed on his next undertaking." No doubt the doctor succeeded, for he died a short time after arriving in California.

Republicans, meanwhile, kept the term "grave robber" politically warm for John Irish, who went on to run unsuccessfully for governor in 1877. In 1880, he moved to California, achieving success and fame in a great many causes for the rest of his life. At his farewell in Iowa City, the citizens gave him a public reception at the St. James Hotel. There, he received a fine gold watch and chain as a testimony of the esteem in which he was held by his friends, both Democrat and Republican.

In Iowa City, the grave-robbing affair was buried and forgotten nearly as quickly as it had arisen. So much so that in March 1871, Issac Potter, one of the students who had assisted with the dissection, quipped at his commencement that "the citizens had watched over the medical institution by night and guarded it by day." The Medical College survived and has since flourished into a globally recognized institution.

For Mrs. Herrick's son, Charles, the incident did not fade. The mutilation done to his mother's body and John Irish's treachery ate at him. Only forty-six years old, he died on May 24, 1871, leaving behind two little sons and his wife, Lizzie, pregnant with a daughter. University of Iowa president Thatcher officiated at his funeral. According to a newspaper account, "When the whole matter was developed before the grand jury and there ignored, his sensitive spirit could not bear up under the sense of wrong and outrage that rested upon him."

A recent walking tour of the older sections of Oakland Cemetery in search of the graves of Mary Herrick and her son Charles produced nothing but consternation. There is no trace of their graves. A sexton even checked through the database and found no record. While it is possible that the Herrick family might have decided it could not trust Oakland Cemetery, the published account of Charles's death states, "He sank rapidly, and quickly found release from the horrid spectre of his outrages and mutilated mother, and he now lies in peace by her side."

Yet 140 years later, Iowa City's most celebrated cadaver is still missing.

LEG BONES EMBEDDED IN A TREE?

The Medical College's early taste for grave robbing was sometimes less than tidy. On January 24, 1913, the *Telegraph-Herald* ran the story of a gruesome discovery by Martin Klome. Klome had been hired to cut down a tree in a grove in the back of Oakland Cemetery. As he split open a trunk, he discovered that the skeletal remains of a human leg from the knee down had been encased inside the wood. The paper conjectured that the bones had been inside the tree for twenty or thirty years.

How did the bones get there? Did heinous experiments by the university's Botany Department produce carnivorous man-eating trees?

One grisly possibility is that perhaps some medical students robbing a grave only needed the torso for their studies. With a sharp shovel and some knowledge of anatomy, it would be a simple task to sever a limb with a well-placed thrust. In the dark of night, with panic muddling their thoughts, they might have tossed the unneeded arms and legs into the adjacent woods.

Unlikely as it sounds, a severed leg might have caught in the branches of a young tree. As other trees and bushes pressed against the branches, they might have twisted and grown tightly against one another, entombing the leg bones between them.

...Or it could have just been experimental carnivorous man-eating trees!

THE HAUNTING OF CURRIER HALL

Cast back your mind to late September 1945. The Second World War has just ended, and you, a fine, strapping blond farm lad from Decorah, Iowa, have just arrived at your dormitory room on the first residential floor at Currier Hall at the University of Iowa in Iowa City. Your roommate, Bob, an athletic, raven-haired youth from bustling Moline, Illinois, helps you get your gear stowed. At last, your empty trunk stands by the door waiting to be taken to storage. With the war over, neither of you is needed to serve your country in combat. For the moment, only one theatre of campaign interests you: women.

Soon, you and Bob are climbing the main staircase to the attic floor. More than once, you or Bob stumble as your eyes meet those of a pretty coed. Though men have been allowed to live in Currier since June 1944, they are still a novelty in this formerly all-women's hall. Shins bruised, you reach the top of the stairway and head to your left down the hall. The air is close and heavy. Though it's late September, summer's heat and humidity make this part of the dorm unbearable. A few paces past the lavatory, you come to a door. It's different than the others in the hall because there's no number over the door. You shove against it, and it opens with a sharp squeal. Inside is an undecorated, brick-walled room piled with trunks and reeking of mothballs. A faint brownish stain on the wood floor catches your eye.

As you lift your trunk onto the stack of others, a loud shriek and bang bursts through the door. Two frisky young blondes enter, laughing over their struggle with an enormous steamer trunk nearly as tall as the door. Without

Currier Hall, built in 1912, was the first women's residential dormitory on the University of Iowa campus. Do the ghosts of a triple suicide haunt its attic floor?

a second thought, you and Bob help the two young women get the big trunk safely stored near the room's single window. When you've finished, they introduce themselves as Doris and Selma.

"We couldn't get it into the elevator," Doris laughs. "So we had to drag it up the stairs. That is the last time I help her with that trunk. It about killed me!"

"Just what I need," Selma complains, "to be haunted by a literature major."

The brown floor stain catches your eye again. You get an idea. "Well, you know, this room is haunted," you carefully observe.

"No, it isn't," Selma chides.

"Really?" Doris asks, her voice sounding wary but intrigued. "A ghost?"

"Actually, there are three," Bob suddenly adds, turning to you and raising his eyebrow, knowingly. "They all died in this very room years ago."

"What malarkey," Selma says.

You point to the dark stain on the wooden floor. "They all killed themselves…in this very room."

"That's why it's only used for trunks now," Bob adds.

Doris fixes you with such a pretty expression that it turns your spine into jelly. "Have you ever seen a ghost?" she asks.

You smile slyly, about to use a real line on a real girl for real for the first time!

"No, but I bet you and I might get lucky if we come here at midnight."

The story of the haunting of Currier Hall might or might not have originated in just that way. Just as the dormitory went through renovations and expansions, so, too, have the two suicide stories. Yet over the intervening years, their central details remain eerily unchanged.

Currier Hall faces the northwest corner of Clinton and Bloomington Streets. Situated on the limestone bluff that overlooks the Iowa River, the dormitory was initially constructed in 1912 to house young women who came to study at the University of Iowa. Though now a U-shaped building, the oldest part of the dormitory is its southeast section and two short wings extending north and west along the two streets. To this day, it retains an august but welcoming appearance.

To augment this augustness, the dormitory was designed according to the British or European practice of designating the floor above the ground floor as the first "story." The ground floor contained the offices, parlors and the dining room. The dormitory rooms began upstairs on the first story (labeled on building plans as "first floor") and continued all the way to the attic floor (labeled on building plans as "fourth floor").

In 1913, 170 women settled into living among the thick carpets and comfortable armchairs set aside warm brick fireplaces in its parlors while paying $22.50 a month for room and ample meals. Dining was a regimented affair. Men in starched white jackets served meals to the residents simultaneously once grace was said. Typical luncheons and dinners consisted of beef, pork and fried chicken. In 1918, however, many residents fell horribly ill in an alarmingly short period. Probably first feared as the Spanish influenza that had ravaged Iowa City that year (killing 38), it soon proved to be a gut-wrenching outbreak of ptomaine poisoning. University president Jessup consequently fired the house director, Mrs. Bella Beard. Angered, Mrs. Beard responded the only way a woman of her unsavory mien could at the time: she served cold pickled cow tongue for her final luncheon.

Tradition has passed down two suicide stories very similar to each other. A 1980s published version of one story is set in the 1910s, but the oldest printed version cites the oral tradition that couches both tales in the 1930s. Even then, the strict rules and regimented behavior were still in effect to protect the safety, security and proprieties of the young women residing there. These rules remained in force until the outbreak of the Second World War. A thirty-two-page book outlined the rules and customs for residents of Currier Hall, covering table manners, behavior to staff and

Parlor of Currier Hall, 1927. *Courtesy of the Frederick W. Kent Collection of Photographs, University of Iowa Libraries, Iowa City, Iowa.*

quiet hours. For example, singing in the bathtub was not allowed. If a woman wanted to bring her own Victrola to play gramophone records, she had to file a petition with the house director and the other residents on her floor. Tap dancing and clogging were also prohibited in any of the rooms. Men were strictly prohibited from being in any of the rooms, with the exception of the parlor on the ground floor. Dancing with men was only allowed there.

Typically, three women shared one room, but single rooms were available. Proctors conducted room checks at 8:00 p.m., knocking at each room and then entering. If the residents were absent, the proctors reported them. The penalties for being absent in the evening grew with each offense. A young woman dallying with a young man and returning late from her rendezvous risked having to spend an evening shut in her room away from her beau. More egregious infractions would see a young woman sequestered in her room for two evenings in a row or longer—perhaps even for eternity.

Valeria's first week at the University of Iowa during that sunny September of 1931 was one of continual discovery. A handsome nineteen-year-old girl, she was a gregarious redhead who made friendships quickly and easily recalled the name of even the slightest acquaintance. She got involved with Currier Hall social events, and through all these, she made discoveries in art, music and ideas that were alien to her small-town Iowa upbringing. She also discovered that she liked smoking and dancing and, occasionally on the weekends, sipped some of the bootleg rye a friend of a friend of a friend quietly brought in from Chicago to a jazz club. Then came the weekend she found herself ensnared in the dark brown eyes of a young writer named William. Her world unraveled.

Valeria forgot about everyone. She stopped writing her weekly letter home. She began spending less time with her friends and lost all interest in Currier's social events. Weekends were devoted to William. Each evening after dinner, she would fuss and primp to prepare for her brief evening with him. Once during the week, she was late getting back. She apologized to the house director, a tolerant matron familiar with young women caught up in university life. She forgave Valeria's infraction and cautioned her to be more mindful.

But as October arrived, Valeria instead became more withdrawn and moody. To her friends, her every waking moment seemed as one long, morose pining for the company of her beau. She soon stopped studying, and her grades suffered. Two more tardy returns to Currier won her one night alone in her room perched all the way up in the attic of Currier. There, she stared out its window down at the slow-moving Iowa River. Another weeknight of dawdling until 11:00 p.m. put her on restriction for two nights in a row; however, she reacted so furiously and rudely that the house director added a third night to her sentence.

One chill Friday evening after dinner, the week before Halloween, Valeria's two best friends complained to her as she stood vigil by the front door watching the street corner. She said nothing, never looked at them and pushed them out of her way to rush through the front door as soon as she saw William. She didn't return until Saturday morning.

Mortified, the house director hauled Valeria to her office. There, she announced that she was writing a letter to Valeria's parents, as well as to the dean of her college, to inform them of the young lady's behavior and recommend that she be expelled from the university if she didn't improve her behavior and respect the house rules forthwith. Before Valeria could respond, the house director told her she would be restricted for the entire week, ending on November 1.

Valeria went to her room in a pure black funk. On Sunday, she came down for meals. On Monday and Tuesday, she was silent. She attended classes and took her meals but stayed as quiet as the grave. From Wednesday to Friday, she complained of being ill and refused to go to class or have meals.

On Saturday, October 31, Valeria said she felt better and came down for breakfast and lunch. The house director allowed her to spend time in the parlor with her friends and other women, but she was not allowed to have any male visitors. As the afternoon wore on, though, it became clear to her friends that Valeria was extremely agitated. She paced the comfortable room nervously, oblivious to the swing music and dramas playing on the radio that enthralled her friends. At last, as the sun set, she returned to her room. She was never seen alive again.

In the morning, she was found dead in a pool of blood. She had cut her own throat with the jagged end of a broken water glass.

Upon the discovery, the house director moved decisively and swiftly. She alerted her superiors. Since it was Sunday, most of the residents had gone to church and other social functions. She helped facilitate discreet visits by senior Iowa City police officers and the county coroner. When the residents arrived in the dining hall, she was able to announce—with complete honesty—that Valeria had decided to leave the university and was on route to her hometown. Her room, meanwhile, was kept locked for the remainder of the academic year, only to be refurbished during the summer.

The fall of 1932 brought a fresh crop of young women to Currier Hall. The young blonde with darting blue eyes who moved into the newly refurbished room in the attic was named Primrose. Originally from Peoria, Illinois, she had a cynical nature that came from being very attractive. The house director at first feared she would have to spray pesticide to drive away Primrose's swarm of suitors. But the young woman quickly demonstrated that she had kept a good head on her shoulders by quickly dismissing all swaggering Don Juans, fawning Romeos and the smoothest of Casanovas. She was active in Currier's social scene, preferred piano sonatas to jazz and sang in a local church choir. It seemed to most of her friends that a straighter, more sensible arrow had never existed in God's quiver.

Or at least it seemed so until early October, when Primrose dropped her pencil at the university library. A young man returned it to her. His name was William, and he was a writer with deep, dark eyes.

Primrose fell apart. She could not keep away from William. She routinely stayed out past the 8:00 p.m. curfew. When she returned, she would push aside the proctor and lock herself in her room. During the last week of October, the house director confronted Primrose at the entrance to the dining hall. Primrose ignored her and pushed past the older woman.

Enraged, she summarily sentenced Primrose to evening confinement in her room for the remainder of the week. That night, Primrose climbed out her window onto the roof, broke through another resident's window and snuck out of the building. She stayed out all weekend and did not return until Monday morning, Halloween.

At that point, the house director had had enough. Cornering the woman in the entrance, she told Primrose that she had consulted with the women's dean and they had decided to suspend her enrollment at the university. She was to pack her things immediately and prepare to go back home on the evening train. Primrose stormed up the stairs, screaming all the way to her room that she would never leave. Of course, she didn't.

The house director made the grisly discovery a little after 8:00 p.m. when she entered the darkened room and turned on the light. Though the light fixture had been torn out from the ceiling and dangled by its wires, it illuminated the room with a raw, jagged glare. Primrose had tried to hang herself with a silken dress belt threaded through the light fixture. She had stood on a bentwood chair and kicked it aside during her attempt. But an instant later, the fixture tore from the ceiling under her weight. Down she crashed on top of the chair, splitting its back and splaying the slats like claws. Two of these broken slats pierced either side of her throat, staking her to the chair. She bled to death.

Again, the house director bridled her horror with discretion. With the quiet influence of her superiors, she quietly alerted the city authorities. The police and coroner arrived quietly, assessed the scene quietly, removed the body quietly and withdrew quietly. At dinner that evening, all the residents already knew that Primrose had been expelled. Having nothing to announce, the house director remained as quiet as the grave.

Once again, the room was kept locked until summer, when it was aired out, cleaned and refurbished. Magnolia moved into it that September 1933. Only eighteen, athletic and giggly, she had sandy hair, green eyes and freckled skin from too much time under the summer sun fussing over her family's livestock. Her attention to the chickens and hogs was not without rewards, for she had won many ribbons at the county fair and several at the Iowa State Fair as well. She proudly displayed these in her room above her bed. The house director grew very fond of Magnolia and watchful, because she entertained a strange fear for Magnolia being alone in her particular room. But as October began, Magnolia's cheerful demeanor remained unchanged. In fact, she seemed to giggle more than before. The house director pushed her fears to the back of her mind.

But Magnolia hadn't told anyone she had met a young writer with deep, dark eyes.

By the middle of the month, Magnolia had gone from being energetic to frenetic. She chattered to herself incessantly and had taken to carrying a little pair of scissors with her. She used these to cut little ribbons of paper, which she scattered in clumps around the parlors on the ground floor. Her friends worried among themselves but let it go no further. All in all, Magnolia observed the house rules, was never late and was never rude to the staff.

The Sunday night before Halloween, the proctor found that Magnolia had not returned to her room. On Monday morning, just as she reported this to the house director, harsh shrieking and shrill laughter erupted from the parlor down the hall. When the two women arrived, they found Magnolia armed with a pair of dressmaker's sheers cutting the long window drapes into ribbons. As soon as she saw the house director, Magnolia dropped the shears and burst into maniacal laughter.

The house director took the unhinged girl up to her dorm room and waited with her until the doctor arrived. The doctor quickly diagnosed stress and exhaustion and injected a sedative into the girl. Magnolia promptly fell asleep. The next day, Halloween, Magnolia seemed normal. Embarrassed and confused, she apologized profusely to the house director. The older woman said they would discuss the damage later but that Magnolia needed distraction and recommended that she take the day off from her classes and relax. Magnolia did just that, returning to lunch with her friends in the dining hall and then leaving again shortly afterward. Dinner, however, was a different story.

Magnolia burst into the dining hall shrieking and laughing, waving a fireplace poker above her head. As the stunned residents watched, she ran up to the jack-o'-lantern set on a table in the middle of the hall and beat it to paste. Without another sound, she darted out of the hall and up the stairs to her room.

Nearly half an hour later, the house director and two proctors arrived at Magnolia's door. They could see light from under the door, but only silence greeted them when they knocked. Using a proctor's key, the house director entered the room by herself.

Bloody streaks covered the walls, window, bedsheets, floor and dresser mirror. The red, raw figure lay in a naked, crumbled heap on the floor. A man's straight razor was held in its hand, and a pile of gore-smeared strips of skin lay near its terrible, grimacing face. When the house director realized that Magnolia had cut herself to ribbons, the horror drove the woman to her knees with weeping.

Once again, influential superiors interceded. The acquiescing city authorities quietly went about their quiet business, and the body quietly returned home. The room, meanwhile was quietly sealed until summer to be refurbished—or so it seemed. When custodians began cleaning the room, the blood on the walls and floor would not wash off. In fact, the more they scrubbed and scoured, the worse it became, until the plaster walls practically ran with blood. With the custodians complaining that the room was cursed, the house director could no longer bear her position and quit. The influential superiors, who would not enter the dormitory, ordered that the walls be bricked over and the new house director find some other purpose for the room. Shortly afterward, the number was taken down from above the door and the room was converted to storage for trunks.

Possibly the newer of the two suicide stories, the next version features a denouement that some have interpreted as being tacked on in the 1960s. Whether the observation is true or not, this version is the best known and most popular of the Currier Hall stories. One wag once quipped that it was a feminist fable, for it warns against men, as well as the distrust and pettiness among women who share their lives in one small dorm room. After all, if three women can't trust and confide with one another while sharing a single room in this life, they might be doomed to do so in the next.

When Adel, Adair and Massena first met in their attic dorm room in Currier Hall that September 1934, they could not have seemed further apart. Adel, the tall, pale blonde, came from a farm near Norway, Iowa. Adair, the stocky one with blazing red hair and freckles, came from a small town in southern Missouri. And Massena, the short, olive-complexioned brunette who swore in Italian, came from Chicago. And yet, almost immediately, the three women got on like a house afire. It wasn't so much that their backgrounds were different as that their preferences in music, fashion, learning and, of course, men complemented one another precisely—so completely, in fact, that they readily finished one another's sentences. Naturally, with any close friendship, conversations that were full of dreams, hopes and confessions often lasted deep into the night. One can but guess what secrets they shared

Three Currier girls in a student room, 1916. *Courtesy of the Frederick W. Kent Collection of Photographs, University of Iowa Libraries, Iowa City, Iowa.*

with one another, but this sharing bound them closely together. Their neighbors across the hall jokingly said the three "were of one mind," and the proctor in charge of that floor called them the "Attic Trinity."

Yet when Adel came running into the room just a few minutes before 8:00 p.m. one night in early October, it heralded disaster for this beautiful friendship. She was unusually delighted and hummed happily to herself, almost to the point of obnoxiously daring her roommate to ask why she was so happy.

Massena cut to the chase, saying to Adair, "It's a boy."

"Well, it sure wasn't that algebra exam," Adair complained. "Our crib sheets were wrong."

"I couldn't help that!" Adel returned dismissively. "Those were the answers I got from him."

"Ah ha!" Massena shouted triumphantly. "So it is a boy! What's his name?"

Adair chimed in, "Come on, dear, spill it."

Adel shook her head, smiling, and sat down on her bed.

"Why not?" demanded Massena. "What's the big secret?"

Adel shook her head again.

"Hey! What gives? Don't you trust us?" Adair complained even louder. "We gotta right, don't we?"

Up to that very instant, Adel had been just about to blurt out all the details of her beau. But her friends' curiosity felt more like prying. Indignation wiped the smile from her lips. She suddenly shouted, "What right? What makes you think you need to know about every minute of my life? Since when did you become my parents?"

"Oh, come off it," snapped Massena. "We always share our secrets."

"Well, not this time," Adel answered curtly. She kicked off her shoes and flung herself down on her bed, facing away from her roommates.

A few days later, Adel still had not spoken one word to her roommates. In fact, as she sat on her bed reading, she had just resolved not to speak to them for the rest of the semester when the door banged open. In charged Massena, holding her books tightly across her chest, looking angry and defiant.

"Why not?" pleaded Adair as she entered the room.

"Because it's none of your business!" Massena snapped. "Leave me alone!"

Adair folded her arms and regarded Adel with the same conspiratorial smirk shared by district attorneys. "She's got herself a boyfriend and won't spill the beans."

Adel sighed loudly and returned to her reading.

"Adel!" Adair whined. "Back me up! We can't let her do this to us!"

"Why not?" Adel said without looking up. "It's her life, she can do what she wants."

"Thank you," Massena returned.

"Wow, gratitude from a two-faced chiseler," Adel spat back.

"Now see here, Adel!" Massena barked.

"What? It's okay for you to go prying into my affairs," Adel said, "but when the shoe's on the other foot it's a different story?"

"So now you've got your nerve back to speak up as the high and mighty one? *Strega! Va fongool!*" Massena shot back and bit her thumb at both women. They promptly left in disgust.

Several nights passed by. In their attic room, the tension was so thick it could be cut for quilt batting to ward off the cold shoulders the three roommates showed one another. On Tuesday evening, the night before Halloween, though, Massena and Adel settled into their beds, assiduously ignoring each other but both noting with some concern that it was almost

10:30 and Adair had not yet returned. At once, they heard the proctor's key turning in their door, and in walked Adair, radiant and beaming, though her hair was disheveled and grass stains covered her elbows.

Adel and Massena looked at each other and then at Adair, who was smiling with all the delight of a cat that had caught a canary. Adel had only parted her lips to speak when Adair cut her off with a very self-satisfied, "No, it's none of your business!" And with that, she got ready for bed.

Not one of them fell asleep when the lights went out. In fact, within an hour and a half, they found themselves comparing notes on their boyfriends. Adel dreamily raved that hers was a writer with dark, soulful eyes. Massena bragged that hers was handsome and dapper and understood what was really happening in Europe. Adair giggled that hers was a passionate brown-eyed devil whom she couldn't resist. Yet while all three laughed at Adair's statement, both Adel and Massena felt slightly unnerved but said nothing. In a moment, they each shrugged it off. After all, what boyfriend wasn't a passionate, irresistible devil?

In the clear light of dawn, they were once more fast friends. They went to breakfast together, attended a lecture together and had lunch together. Their neighbors, who had scrupulously avoided being drawn into the crossfire of their friends' troubles, came out of the woodwork, happy to see the three were again one. There was talk of the dorm's Halloween party that night and plans to carve some pumpkins for the dining hall. It should have continued happily onward but for a fateful decision: all three women decided they would surprise their boyfriends as they left their 3:30 class on the Pentacrest.

At 3:30 p.m., all three women stood in front of the Old Capitol straining their heads toward Schaeffer Hall, eager to meet their very own beau and show him off to their roommates. It seemed an eternity for each until at last a tall, dapper-dressed young man emerged from the north entrance of the building and paused to straighten his tie.

Adel, Adair and Massena called out at once:

"William, dearest!"

"Over here, darling!"

"Come here, honey! Look, I brought some friends!"

The young man looked at them, and for a moment, a shadow of alarm raced across his face. Then, he abruptly walked up to them and said, "Good afternoon, ladies." But he didn't do it in a gentlemanly sort of way. He pronounced the word "ladies" as "laid-ease." Then he topped it off with a sneering grin before turning on his heel and hiking briskly away.

Special permission had been granted Currier Hall residents to be out late from their rooms because of the Halloween costume party on the ground floor. Women were allowed to bring guests, including sweethearts, to the opulent parlors. Because of the throng, many of the revelers didn't realize until late that none of the three friends ever came down.

It wasn't until those late, dark hours when the powers of evil are exalted that the proctor's keys clattered in the attic room's lock. Whether it was by poison, rope or blade is never mentioned, but the proctor found them in a ghastly tableau of death. Each had taken her own life.

The triple suicide threatened a public relations nightmare for the university. Currier's staff moved quickly to expunge all trace of the horror. And to further guard against memory of the event, the attic room was converted to storage space and its number removed. Yet in spite of all the university's cleaning and concealing, it's still said that when Currier Hall roommates fight, three shadowy women appear and counsel them to get along.

Are the tales true? An examination of the building's architecture and history, as well as Iowa City's news archives, makes the suicides highly unlikely. On blueprints and in the dormitory's guidebooks, the room was used for storing trunks that helped transport the belongings of the first women to live here. In that time, the room had no number. When Currier's south wing was expanded in 1939, the room continued unnumbered. Later, in the 1940s, as trunks gave way to smaller luggage, the space was used for storing anything from spare chairs to mattresses, desks and even carpet scraps. Throughout that time, the room had no number. In fact, it wasn't until the final northern addition was completed in 1949 that the room received a number, E407. Even then, plans still labeled it as a trunk room.

Yet between 1939 and 1949, a dark, selfish force impudently penetrated the deepest recesses of Currier Hall on such a scale that had never before been permitted in this women's bastion. On June 1, 1944, men moved in.

Given that the stories are about young women, love, virtue and death and occur in an unnumbered room in the highest part of the women's dormitory, one cannot but revel in this romantic gambit's gothic overtones. They offer so much more than "Come here often, sweetheart?"

Over time, the location of the suicide floor has confused many people who are unfamiliar with Currier's esoteric floor-numbering system. In the 1960s

CURRIER HALL: Plan of the fourth floor. The floors are connected by elevator.

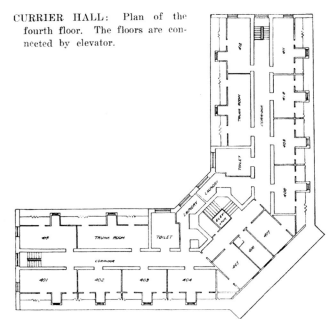

Left: Plan of the fourth floor, Currier Hall, 1918. *Courtesy of Buildings and Grounds Vertical Files Collection, University of Iowa Libraries, Iowa City, Iowa.*

Below: Completion of the final expansion phase. Plan of the fourth floor, Currier Hall, 1949. *Courtesy of Buildings and Grounds Vertical Files Collection, University of Iowa Libraries, Iowa City, Iowa.*

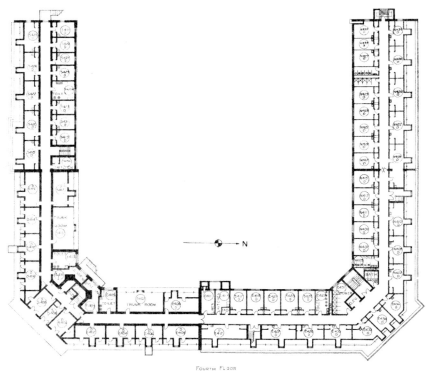

FOURTH FLOOR

and 1970s, a popular bloody dorm story ending with the line "Aren't you glad you turned on the light?" made its way through the Midwest and was adapted to Currier Hall. This urban myth appears in Jan Harold Brunvand's *The Vanishing Hitchhiker*. In 1980, when *The Shining* began showing in theatres before Halloween, residents on the fourth floor (third story) mischievously placed a sign reading REDRUM in a window facing the busy intersection. Consequently, students seeing the sign came to think that the famed suicide room was on the fourth floor—not the fourth story. While this example might seem a frivolous splitting of hairs, it's a detail that makes chasing down the haunting of Currier Hall much like chasing…well, a ghost.

To this day, though, Currier Hall residents in the upper stories say their closet doors close and open by themselves, their lights flicker oddly and dresser drawers slam shut. Several have reported sudden cold spots in un-air-conditioned areas during the summertime. At least once, a paranormal investigator journeyed across the state from Des Moines at the request of one frightened resident. Undoubtedly, Currier Hall is haunted, but whether it is by a good yarn, student angst or troubled forces scarcely understood in this world cannot be conclusively established.

Perhaps some late October night, you might get to investigate the story of Currier's fourth story. The famed suicide room is located on the fourth story (the attic floor—or in good ol' American terms, the fifth floor). Take the main elevator to the fourth story, turn left and head past the restroom. It is the next door on the left.

Perhaps you'll even get lucky.

THE ALAMO HOUSE HAUNTING

In 2004, Shirley and Ray Hendrickson bought an unusual home at 228 Brown Street. Built in 1908 and listed on the National Registry of Historic Places in 1986, the house was built in the Mission style of the American Southwest. Complete with terra cotta tile roof and stucco walls, it featured distinctive Spanish colonial–style dormers that once earned it the nickname "The Alamo."

In 2005, the couple had just completed renovating and restoring the house and had opened it as the Mission House Bed and Breakfast. One day, Ray was mowing the lawn out front. As he made a pass along the side of the house, a younger man on a bicycle pulled over and said quite earnestly, "You know this house is haunted."

Ray asked him to explain, but the man said he didn't know much about it save that he had heard that the house was haunted. Ray shared the story with Shirley, and they both grinned, rolled their eyes and thought nothing more about it. After all, it was an old home in a very old neighborhood.

What the two didn't know was that about 1985, the house was not just haunted—it was very haunted. So very haunted, in fact, that the people involved with the episode still refuse to talk about the house.

The early to mid-1980s saw the bottom years for homes in the historic Brown Street neighborhood. The neighborhood had been spiraling into the student housing morass for over a decade. As the last few homeowners aged, their homes fell into disrepair. Enterprising (and typically absentee)

228 North Brown Street, the Arthur Hillyer Ford House. Once known by some as the Alamo and thought to be haunted, it is now the Mission House Bed and Breakfast.

landlords snapped up these houses, carved them up into apartments and rented them to college students.

One was 228 Brown Street. By the mid-1980s, the house had faded from its glory years. Cracks and holes scarred the faded stucco. Weeds had sprouted in spaces left by missing roof tiles. Bathed in the light of an October moon, the house glowed like a pile of raw bone. Drunken students staggering home from downtown bars shuddered at this decrepit house and hurried away.

An out-of-town doctor who already owned several other student rental houses in Iowa City bought the house late in 1984. He decided to make some repairs and improvements, but primarily he wanted to subdivide the house to accommodate more tenants. He planned on cutting in a second entrance on the stairway, walling off the parlor into its own apartment, adding a kitchenette to the second floor and subdividing more rooms as well.

The details are sketchy, having come from multiple reluctant sources, but it's safe to say that the contractor who took the job may have known that he and his crew faced a terrible challenge. The original interior of the house had been finished in the Craftsman style by experts. The foyer featured hardwood pocket doors inlaid with narrow strips of ebony and basswood. A double-grooved plate rail extended around the dining room, and along its west wall, the massive radiator had a bread-warming cage built into it. The high ceilinged parlor featured an intimate inglenook, a pair of small facing benches flanking the red-bricked fireplace. Hardwood flooring ran throughout. One of the university's legendary football heroes, Nile Kinnick, had even lived in the house during the historic 1938 and 1939 football seasons. In essence, the workers' job was to carve up this lovely historic home. They might not have liked the job, but that was the job they were being paid to do.

At first, work in the house went along without incident. Then, odd things began happening with the electrical system. Power tools would turn on and off without any reason. Checking over the fuse panels showed nothing wrong with the old screw-in-style bus fuses. All the same, new fuses were installed, but very shortly, the problems would happen again. Tools would vanish from one room and show up in another. Of course, this was dismissed as forgetfulness, and the work went on. That is, until something really weird began happening.

The foyer of 228 North Brown Street.

The inglenook and parlor of 228 North Brown Street.

One day, three of the carpenters were working upstairs in the kitchenette. All three were in their late twenties and were known to be conscientious about doing a professional job. Nothing out of the ordinary seemed to happen until they all suddenly realized they were standing downstairs on the main floor staring at the empty wall in front of them. Not only that, but an hour had passed since the time they recalled being upstairs! None of them knew at all how they got to be on the main floor.

The three kept it under their hats, but when the same thing happened to others on the crew, they told their boss. Perhaps he thought it was a joke being played on him. Perhaps he later thought it was just the flu going around and making his men feel dizzy. Then, he came by the house one day to check on some repair work being done on an upstairs ceiling joist. The man who was supposed to be fixing it was nowhere to be seen. The boss called and shouted for the man but got no response. He went down to the main floor and looked for him there, making a ruckus as he went, but he still couldn't find him. Finally, recalling the problems with the fuses, the boss went down into the basement. There he found his carpenter just standing next to a wall. He shouted at the man, but his carpenter did nothing. Finally, the boss grabbed his shoulder and shook him. The man started suddenly at the sight of his boss and then looked around the room. "How'd I get here?" he asked.

The next morning, the crew showed up at the house and refused to work until something was done to stop the bizarre occurrences. After some time, they agreed to return to work only after a priest came to the house and blessed it. After a day or two, the blessing took place and the carpenters returned to work. No further incidents happened.

So what really happened? Groups of grown men don't drops their tools and walk off a job just because of a couple of finicky circuit fuses. Nor do they risk their professional reputations as craftsmen in a highly competitive market by mixing hallucinatory drugs with dangerous power tools or making up stories about lost time. Clearly, these men experienced something truly strange.

The shocking coincidence is the house's history. On the National Register of Historic Places, the house's official name is the Arthur Hillyer Ford House, after the man who had it built, Professor Arthur Hillyer Ford, the first head of the University of Iowa Electrical Engineering Department. Professor Ford was born in Chicago in 1874. He got his start in electrical engineering when the industry as we know it today was just in its infancy. He earned his bachelor's degree from the University of Wisconsin in 1895 and went on to hold fellowships at the University of Wisconsin and also Columbia University. He consulted with electrical companies in Schenectady, New York, Chicago and New York City. He then went on to teach at the University of Colorado and Georgia Tech. Ford's work with transformers was an important component for the industry to bring efficient and affordable electricity into the American home.

In 1905, at the age of thirty-one, Professor Ford became the head of the Electrical Engineering Department at the University of Iowa. One of his first tasks was to design the electrical equipment for the hydroelectric plant to power the university when the first roller dam was built under Burlington Street in 1906.

It is evident from his academic career and his missionary work as a Congregationalist that Professor Ford enjoyed traveling. Doubtless, he was very influenced by the American Southwest. On June 18, 1908, he married Sadie Murray Hess of Iowa City. The two honeymooned for six months while their singular and unique home was built for them on Brown Street. They soon had three children, Ellen, Edwin and Robert, and the couple seemed to take them everywhere, including a trip from Iowa City to Fort Lauderdale, Florida, to see Professor Ford's mother in 1923. The Ford family drove the entire distance and enjoyed the adventure.

Professor Ford's later work included electrical power transmission in Iowa, electromagnetism and commercial telephone transmitters. He also wrote about and gave presentations on street lighting and store lighting. He met students with different viewpoints on the use of electricity. One of these was a young student named Donald Lindsley. Lindsley would later go on to become one of the first scientists to use electroencephalography, or EEG, to record electrical brain activity. Lindsley would also marry Professor Ford's daughter, Ellen, in 1933.

Unfortunately, Professor Ford never saw that day. He died in 1930 at the age of fifty-six. His wife, Sadie, continued on in the house for many years. One way she supplemented her income was to take in student boarders. This included renting space in her home to the Phi Kappa Psi fraternity as an annex. One of her boarders was Nile Kinnick. In 1957, Sadie grew too old to care for the home, and she moved away. She died in 1963. The home passed through two other families until that fateful year of 1985.

Was the professor still protecting his dream home fifty-five years after his death? Was the spirit of a man who manipulated electrical energy in life using the same forces to preserve his home in death? Were the carpenters' bouts of missing time the result of electroshock delivered by this guardian spirit? Or was it just an old house plagued with cheap fuses and perhaps even a rare mold or fungus infestation that caused hallucinations? Decide for yourself—but remember that something drove a full crew of hourly paid professional carpenters to walk off a job and not reenter until the house had been exorcised. And to this day, not one of them will speak of it.

Except for a writer who asked odd questions, Shirley and Ray Hendrickson say they have had no odd occurrences. They have felt no cold drafts, heard no footsteps, seen no vague shadows and had no complaints of such from anyone who has stayed with them. The electrical service has been renovated and is reliable. They have also been lucky to have visits from the Fords' grandchildren. Maybe part of the reason they have no problems is that Shirley and Ray have restored the once scary old Alamo house to what it must have been like when Professor Ford and Sadie were alive. Clearly, the two have invested a lot of time and money in the home as a bed-and-breakfast business, but it also speaks volumes to their commitment to architecture, history and preservation in one of Iowa City's most historic neighborhoods.

You could even say 228 Brown Street has become their Mission House.

MAUDE THE GHOST

In 1998, the Alderman-Wilson Insurance Group merged with Welt, Ambrisco, Winegarten Insurance and moved to a new, spacious office building on Westside Drive. The merger ended the A.W. Insurance Group's forty-three years at 319 East Bloomington Street. Apart from giving up a historic 1870s brick house in the Northside business area of Iowa City, A.W. Insurance also gave up the ghost. That is, the ghost named Maude.

Right off, it's not exactly clear who Maude was or is or how she came to be. For as long as A.W. Insurance had been at the house on Bloomington Street, it seemed that Maude had been there. In fact, Maude might have been invented by the company's staff as a workplace joke. Since the house was an old Victorian, it seemed fitting that it should have a ghost. So when staff mislaid pens or markers or other office supplies, Maude caught the blame. If one of the staff forgot about setting aside a client folder in an odd place to answer a phone call, Maude caught the blame. If the building creaked and groaned at night when staff worked late in the building, they would say Maude was being restless. Or if they heard muffled voices they thought came from people walking past the building outside, they would say Maude was nagging them to go home.

In all likelihood, Maude would have quietly faded from memory as most workplace jokes do—except that she actually appeared.

The story comes from one of the former co-owners of the business, Don Flack. One day about 1988, one of the senior agents was standing within arm's reach of the first-floor bathroom. She was a well-respected middle-

319 East Bloomington Street, the Graf House. Did Anna Graf's ghost finally get so sick and tired of being called "Maude" that she appeared?

aged woman known for her professionalism and her no-nonsense attitude. She was speaking with one of the other agents when she casually glanced into the bathroom and saw an elderly woman in an old-style dress standing in front of the mirror with her arms raised to fix her hair, which was also done up in an old-fashioned style. The senior agent thought nothing about it at first and continued her conversation for a moment or two. Something didn't seem right to her, so she glanced back behind her at the bathroom—but this time the elderly woman was gone.

Since she was only standing about three feet away from the bathroom door, she knew that she would have seen anyone trying to leave the bathroom. They would have run right into her. Keeping this observation to herself for the moment, she asked the agent she was speaking with to enter the bathroom to see if anyone was inside. Confused, the agent entered and switched on the light but found the little room empty.

At that moment, Don Flack entered the scene and asked what had happened. The senior agent was clearly upset and flustered, for she was certain that she had seen something that was clear as day one moment and gone the next. Years later, Don said after telling the story, "After talking with her and listening to her explain what happened, I do believe she saw something. She was not one of those that would take the time to make it up."

So, then, who is Maude?

The secret may lie in that sudsy golden elixir that made Iowa City famous in the late nineteenth century: beer.

Simeon Hotz was born in 1819 in Fuetzen, Baden (Germany). Having served as a soldier in Brentano's revolutionary army in 1848, he fled to the United States like many other Germans at the time (including Brentano). Arriving in Iowa City, he at first worked as a shoemaker and then as a grocer. In 1852, he met and married the widow Mrs. Barbara Williams. The couple would have eight children, two of whom were daughters, Clara and Anna.

In 1853, Louis Englert persuaded Hotz to leave the grocer's shelves for the brewer's tun. City Brewery at 315 Market Street (the block to the south of Bloomington Street) brewed about ten barrels a day using a single brass kettle. By 1857, Hotz had learned enough of the art to set out to make beer on his own. The Civil War, however, interrupted both Englert's and Hotz's foamy endeavors, and neither man returned to beer making until after the war. In 1868, Hotz teamed up with Anton Geiger and established the Union Brewery (also known as the Geiger-Hotz Brewery) on the corner of Market and Linn Streets, just across the alley from St. Mary's Catholic Church. The brewery building still stands and is a large three-story brick building, 160 feet long by 50 feet wide. When the brewery's foundation was dug, caves were found. These were lined with brick and used to store barrels of beer. Meanwhile, Anton Geiger later married Hotz's daughter Clara, and in 1870 the two built a grand Anglo-Italian-style house at 213 Market Street, just a few yards west of the brewery.

Meanwhile, Englert's brewery stood just half a block east of Hotz's Union Brewery. Both operated saloons. Englert's was located at the front of the brewery at Market Street, and Hotz's saloon and hotel stood at the southeast corner of Linn and Market Streets, just across the street from his brewery.

Fortunately for Hotz, Conrad Graf, a twenty-five-year-old experienced brewmaster, arrived in 1874. Hotz put him in charge of making beer. Within a year, Graf married his boss's other daughter, Anna. The couple then bought the beautiful new Anglo-Italian-style home across the block at 319 East Bloomington Street.

In 1877, Englert sold out his brewery to his son, John J. Englert, and son-in-law and went into the ice and lumber business. Hotz's brewery prospered, and things looked good for the extended Hotz family until tragedy struck in 1881, when Simeon Hotz died. Graf eventually took over running the brewery, expanding production to fifty barrels a day (approximately fourteen thousand a year) and installed steam heat. At one point, Graf's Brewery, as it became known, owned several buildings on Linn, Market and Bloomington Streets.

Meanwhile, the huge Great Western Brewery run by another German, John Dostal, had opened up at the east end of the block at Market and Gilbert Streets. Thus, the single 300 block Market Street shared three giants in beer making: Graf's, Englert's City Brewery and Dostal's Great Western. It looked like the business of Iowa beer had found a place to mature and age.

In fact, it was a powder keg. Iowa City mirrored the rest of the state and was deeply divided by the issue of prohibition. The battle lines were drawn along ethnicity, class, religion and politics. Most brewers and their customers in Iowa were working-class German immigrants, usually Catholic and Democrats. Those who looked down on them tended to be native-born Anglo-Irish American professionals (involved in law, medicine or publishing), Protestant and Republicans who backed the temperance movement and supported prohibition.

In 1882, the Iowa legislature passed an amendment to the Iowa Constitution that prohibited all alcohol. The amendment was submitted to voters on June 27, 1882, and it passed 155,430 to 125,677. However, the Koehler and Lange Brewery of Davenport filed a suit contending that the amendment was invalid because it had not passed in the same form in both sessions of the legislature. The Iowa Supreme Court found in favor of the brewer, and the amendment was voided. Undeterred, the temperance-controlled Iowa legislature bounced back with a series of laws prohibiting the manufacture, transport or sale of liquor. These laws took effect on July 4, 1884.

All across the state, brewers found that all their inventory—thousands, if not millions, of gallons of beer in barrels and bottles—was suddenly illegal and prohibited for sale. They were also faced, along with saloonkeepers, with being put out of work and possibly held criminally liable for possession with intent to sell. Naturally, enforcement of the law proved another matter. County supervisors still granted permits for saloons. In Dubuque and Sioux City, the law was largely ignored. Iowa City, meanwhile, struggled with its drinking.

On July 14, an Iowa City saloon owner unceremoniously tapped a keg to protest the new law. A crowd gathered and soon grew so large that drinkers had to wait in line thirty minutes for beer. After officers arrested the owner and locked up the saloon, the mob broke into the saloon by throwing empty kegs through the windows. Once they discovered the beer was kept locked in the cellar, they forced the brewer to come with the keys to open it. The bacchanal continued until even the dregs were drained.

On July 25, Johnson County sheriff Fletcher served an injunction from Judge Christian Hedges of the circuit court (a revered Republican judge) on Conrad Graf, forbidding him from keeping and maintaining a place for the illegal manufacture and sale of liquors. Dostal probably received a similar notice, and both brewers very likely tore them to tatters and were promptly cited.

On August 13, Conrad Graf and John Dostal were on their way to their trial for violating the new liquor laws. A crowd of 150 men followed them four and a half miles out of town to the home of a justice of the peace named John Schell. Once there, the mob attacked the prosecuting attorneys, William Bailey and L.G. Swafford. Graf's bartender caught Swafford by the throat, allowing the mob to beat the man, strip off his clothes and then coat him with tar. A constable surnamed Parrot, who had also filed liquor charges against Graf and Dostal, was stabbed in the thigh and struck in the head. The mob brought out ropes and began screaming to hang the constable and attorney A.E. Maine, both of whom took refuge in the house. Rioters pulled out their revolvers and started shooting into the house and throwing stones, terrifying Mrs. Schell, her children and her very ill mother. The rioting continued for several hours with both Graf and John J. Englert, a city council member, urging the mob on. By evening, the mob had dispersed back into town.

The riot lit up the telegraph lines coast to coast. Newspapers from Paterson, New Jersey, to Salt Lake City, Utah, ran the story. Iowa City officials dragged their heels at arresting anyone primarily because one of the mob's ringleaders sat on city council. Finally, Judge Hedges issued warrants for the arrest of Graf, Englert and Dostal. When a grand jury was empanelled in Iowa City to consider the criminal liquor charges against Graf et al, it refused to indict anyone. A civil suit, meanwhile was filed by the beaten and tarred Swafford, claiming $20,000 in damages. The venue was changed to Marengo and then to Marion because no impartial jury could be found.

To make matters worse, while waiting for the suit to come to trial, Graf could not keep his anger under control. On May 13, 1885, he assaulted William Bailey in a local park with the aid of his teamster, Charles Sweim. "Bailey's face was pounded almost to a jelly, and there are large lumps under his eyes," the *Cedar Rapids Gazette* correspondent reported. Bailey filed a civil suit two days later against Graf claiming $5,000 damages. The two men were arrested, but the case was later dismissed.

The suit's verdict was handed down on June 3, 1886. The jury found for the plaintiff, Swafford, and awarded him $7,000. The cost seems to have been shared between the brewers.

Graf must have looked at the verdict as a minor setback. He had already managed to get his county permit reinstated under his mother-in-law's name, Barbara Hotz. In reality it was just a matter of time. In 1888, Graf closed the brewery, and for a time he may have relied on the bottling plant and ice business. Then, in 1893, the U.S. Supreme Court declared the Iowa law a violation of the Commerce Clause. Graf reopened his brewery at full throttle.

On November 16, 1894, Graf went to bed complaining of bronchitis. He was found dead the next morning at the age of forty-five. He left his wife, Anna, and their three teenage sons to run the family businesses. In 1896, Chris Senner, who had been a manager of the brewery sometime before, returned to resume his old job. Soon, he married Anna Graf. In 1903, the brewery was taken over by Graf's three sons and renamed Graf Brothers. William Robert Graf later bought out his brothers' interests, only to be forced to close the brewery in 1916 when Iowa again enacted Prohibition—which lasted until 1933. Anna, having spent several happy years with Senner, died in 1917.

The house was sold after her death. It passed through several different owners over the years, becoming a business office for Measurement Resources Corporation in the early 1970s and even being used as a Jaycee Haunted House for two years. Afterward, it was an antique store briefly and then a home decorating store until A.W. Insurance arrived in 1981 and its staff started blaming things on Maude.

While Anna was active in her later life in the Iowa City card club and St. Mary's Catholic Church, doubtless the social divisions caused by the temperance movement caused her some pain. After all, because of the hard work and colossal success of her father and her two husbands in brewing, she probably should have been accorded the same respect from her Republican peers. More than likely, however, these ladies of the temperance movement saw her as an agent of the sin and social degradation they were fighting. By making beer, she was to blame for the problems of demon alcohol. Moreover, she was German and Catholic. It must have also been extremely frustrating during her first years alone without Conrad, when Iowa City's Republican elected officials may have made things difficult for the brewery to operate. After all, it's conceivable that some blamed her for what Conrad had done to them during the riots of 1884.

Maybe what Don Flack described happening in 1988 was the moment Anna's spirit had had enough. She had been a wealthy and influential lady in the earliest days of Iowa City and had put up with sanctimonious do-gooders blaming her and her family for countless social ills all her life. To be blamed for petty trifles—let alone called by the wrong name—was the absolute last straw. Maybe it was time to remind people who she really was.

And that's what Don Flack's colleague saw that day in 1988: a mature woman of wealth and means calmly arranging her hair in the mirror.

CITY HIGH'S WHISTLING JANITOR

Built in 1937 and recently remodeled, City High can be a nightmare to navigate. To new students and their parents, it can seem like a real-world Escher building: impossible, improbable and incomprehensible. Because of its infuriating twists and turns, some believe that the custodians cleaning at the end of the year routinely discover the mummified remains of freshman students who got lost at the beginning of the year in some forgotten alcove at the end of a hallway.

Not surprisingly, City High has a few haunting stories associated with it. The real guardians of those ghost stories are the custodial staff who are trusted to patrol the corridors, ever on the lookout for matters Hogwartian. According to the current head custodian, George Volk, many stories were passed on to him by a former head named Shorty Goodman, who began his duties in 1965.

One, of course, concerns the bell tower. Some variations tell of a young woman (who is usually described as a student, though sometimes a teacher in order to make it more salacious) who climbed into the bell tower and hanged herself over losing her boyfriend or being rejected by a boy either before or after prom. For years afterward, her tortured soul wandered the school, bewildering the math classes with moans, animating dead frogs in biology and perfuming the boys' locker room with the scent of magnolias.

Unfortunately, this is the urban myth version. After all, think about just how many high schools were built across the country in the 1930s by the Works Progress Administration. Almost every single one of them has

City High School. Are disembodied midnight whistling and the noises in the heating pipes all that remain of janitors who never left?

a bell tower. Besides, bell towers are kept locked because young people enjoy hurling stupid things from great heights, especially if they are runny and smelly or remove paint and especially if the teachers' parking lot is nearby.

The real story about the tower has nothing to do with scorned love. Rather, it is because of heartfelt loss during wartime. During World War II, City High did its part for the war effort like any other American high school, especially since many of the students' fathers were serving overseas. During a scrap metal drive in 1943, City High even pulled its bell out of its tower and sent it off to be scrapped. The following year, 1944, saw some of the harshest fighting on all fronts as America and its allies closed in on their enemies. One student lost his father, killed in action. The student grew morose and depressed. One night, he broke into the high school and climbed into the tower. It was there, from the old bell yoke, that he hanged himself. For ten years afterward, on the anniversary of the father's death, people could hear the bell ring.

Another chief feature of City High is the massive smokestack behind the Opstad Auditorium. Back in Shorty's time, the stack used to be much higher because the school's physical plant burned coal to heat the boilers that made steam to heat the school's radiator system. The stack had to be high enough to ensure that any sparks from the stack would burn out before they dropped to roof level. While the coal-fired boilers are long gone, to this day, students will hear squeals, moans and strange rapping-like sounds in the morning as the system pumps heated steam through the building. According to Shorty, there was a young custodian in the early 1960s whose job was to make sure the furnace was stoked each morning with coal to heat the building. One morning, two tons of coal were delivered to the high school by dumping them down the coal chute into the bunker. When the young custodian arrived, he noticed the building was cold, so he went to the furnace room and found the bunker was piled high with coal. However, the stoker (an auger-like device) had shut down; it wasn't getting any coal from the bunker because the doors were closed. He pulled open the bunker door, and the coal tumbled out into the auger. He started the auger motor, and it began feeding coal into the furnace. Unfortunately, the guy did not know that smoldering coal furnaces can suddenly flash over when the furnace door is suddenly opened. At an ill-chosen moment, he opened the three-foot-diameter furnace door to see why the coal had not ignited. KA-WOOSH went the furnace. The sudden fire created such suction that it pulled the guy inside. In seconds, the terrific heat had burned him to a handful of cinders.

The noises in the steam pipes that students hear each winter morning are the sighs and screams of that janitor's soul trying to escape the school's radiator system. The school's custodians know that one day he will find his way out because the new boiler's safety system utilizes a graduated release.

Still, there is another story that begins in the late 1950s or so, when a middle-aged janitor named Charlie started working at City High. Charlie was very good at his job and helped maintain the boilers, kept the classrooms spotless, helped clean up clumsy spills in the art room and knew exactly what to put on the little piles of spilled powder in the chemical lab so that they wouldn't explode. His nightly rounds took him and his push broom from the top floor of one side of the old building down and around until he finished out by the trash bins at the back. Along the way, he'd check doors, empty wastebaskets and tidy the classrooms. All the while that he was working, he whistled snatches of popular tunes from the 1940s and early '50s. In no time at all, he established an efficient yet comfortable routine that allowed him to finish up well before midnight and let him spend more time at home with his wife.

Unfortunately, all comfortable routines are doomed by change. It was only few years until his experience gained him more responsibilities and longer hours. Gradually, his wife grew more irritated by his longer hours. She nagged and complained that she never saw him and they never went out anymore and would he please not leave his dirty dungarees on the floor when he came home at night.

Some nights, Charlie liked to think she had more in common with a cranky grizzly bear needing an undisturbed night's sleep. So he would stay at the high school, falling asleep in an old office chair he had parked in a corner of the boiler room. At about 4:00 a.m., he'd wake up and make another round through the school. He'd greet the incoming teachers and then head home to sneak in the back door with the morning paper.

Charlie worked for a brief time with Shorty and then retired in the late 1960s. He died soon afterward. Years passed. By the late 1970s, the younger janitors who had worked with Charlie back in the day were well into their middle years themselves. Because City High's students aped the university protests going on, the administration decided on improving building security. A door indicator panel was installed in the janitor's office. It told the custodian the status of every hall door and exit door in the school by lighting up a small lamp: green if a door was open or red if it was closed. By the very tail end of the day, after all the clubs and games had finished, a custodian could just look at the panel to see if all lights were red, indicating all the doors were closed.

Now, the story goes that Shorty was working late one night at City High when he chanced to look over at the panel and saw that one of the lights was green. That was very odd because he was the only one in the building that night and had made sure that all the doors were closed and locked as he made his rounds. He walked all the way across the building and found one of the old hallway doors open. It wasn't hanging wide open, just slightly ajar. Thinking that the latch had failed, he tested it with his finger to make certain it wasn't sticking. The latch moved freely, so Shorty closed the door and headed back to the room to pick up his lavatory cleaning gear.

When he returned to the janitor's office, he saw that the same indicator light was lit up green again. Annoyed, he went back down and found the door slightly ajar again. This time he closed and pushed it slightly to make sure he heard the latch engage, which it did with a sharp click. He went back to the room, and this time the light was red. Satisfied, he headed up to the third floor with his cleaning supplies. As he gained the top of the stairs, though, he heard someone whistling a little jazz tune. He waited a moment, but it faded—not like it was receding into the distance but just getting fainter and fainter.

The first thing that leapt to his mind had to be impossible. Charlie had died years ago. It couldn't be him. It had to be the pipes. Yes, it had to be them. So why were they whistling "String of Pearls"? Shorty heard the whistling again and again over the next few years, and he grew dead certain that he knew to whom it belonged.

Supposedly, one of the other custodians during the 1980s had a similar experience. He heard the whistling more often and louder than other janitors. There were also footsteps and doors slamming. After some months of this, it is said that he quit because he couldn't take it any longer.

The whistling and other noises were last heard about the end of the 1980s or possibly the very early 1990s. Whether the noises came about because of the heating pipes or unknown people in the building at the same time as the janitors can't ever be proved or disproved. But the story goes that both janitors knew Charlie well and both knew the tunes he enjoyed whistling.

If the noises and whistling were in fact Charlie, then why did he stop? Perhaps ghosts get used to comfortable routines—that's why it's called "haunting." Perhaps the end was a result of all the changes to City High: new computer wiring, new gym, more and more students. Maybe the building began to look like it was going to get so complicated that even a ghost could get lost.

On the other hand, maybe he was just avoiding his cranky wife one last time.

OLD BRICK'S CURSE

Every group of people has strong disagreements within itself. Churches seem to be magnets for such trouble because necessity entangles questions of both faith and money. As any of Iowa City's ministers, pastors or priests will privately confess, headstrong members in a congregation make a minister's job of guiding his flock feel more like that of herding cats. In fact, the thing that keeps most clerics tossing in their beds is the hellish threat of a congregational conflict over their money, their minister or their building.

Some folks believe that buildings can be haunted without ghosts. They believe that intense negative human emotions concentrated in one place are absorbed by their environment and then are periodically released, sort of like when intense pressure and energy in a geological fault is released in an earthquake. What these folks contend is that the local area (such as a battlefield or building) replays the events and that the ghostly apparitions one sees in these spectrally conflicted places are not spirits but merely shadows of the life forces imprinted in the place. Like an earthquake, the manifestations can be small tremors or major temblors.

Other folks, however, invoke Charles Dickens's saying that manifestations are perhaps the consequences of an "undigested bit of beef, a blot of mustard, a crumb of cheese, a fragment of underdone potato."

In the case of Iowa City, Old Brick has witnessed congregational conflicts at its location on the northwest corner of Market and Clinton Streets for more than 180 years. Known originally as the North

Presbyterian Church, troubles there began even before the church that preceded it was completely finished—all because of an eccentric but hot-tempered minister and his bell.

HUMMER'S BELL

In August 1840, the Schuyler Presbytery in Illinois appointed the Reverend Michael Hummer as pastor to the new Presbyterian church in Iowa City. He had already had experience starting up churches in Terre Haute, Indiana, and Davenport, Iowa, and was also in the midst of establishing a church in Red Oak, Iowa. By fall, the Schuyler Presbytery had set off nine new Iowa churches on its own. These then formed the Iowa Presbytery, which met and formally organized on November 6, 1840, in Muscatine (which was then known as Bloomington).

Since the Iowa City congregation had no meetinghouse at the time, they used whatever places they could manage, including a schoolhouse, the Mechanic's Academy, Butler's Hotel and the Council Chamber at the Old Capitol. While Hummer was technically the regular pastor, the Iowa Presbytery sent him to the East Coast to raise funds for other Iowa churches. All told, Hummer took three trips and was allowed to keep 10 percent of the money he raised. It was during one of his trips east in 1844 that he contracted with Andrew Meneely (the name originally was McNeely) in West Troy, New York, for the casting of a bell for his church in Iowa City. Hummer paid $500 for the bell. Meneely bells were known to have a superior beauty of tone and had won medals at fairs in New York State. When the bell arrived, it was said to have been placed in a frame and kept just inside the Old Capitol's east door, since they were using the council chamber for meetings.

Hummer's tone, meanwhile, never seemed to be as clear and beautiful. He has been described as brilliant, fiery and imperious. In particular, he was known for a hot temper that he cared little to control. He was also actively pursuing new ideas of spiritualism, including Swedenborgism, which rankled many in his congregation.

In 1846, the Iowa Presbytery sent Hummer east once again to collect money for the building of the Des Moines College and seminary it hoped to construct in Lee County, Iowa, at West Point. (In 1853, the college had forty-five students and three faculty members. By 1865, it had ceased to exist.) Upon his return, some of the congregation began to whisper that their minister had misappropriated funds for his own use. After all, he alone collected the donations for the churches and college, and from these he alone paid his expenses and his salary. No one could verify the amount he collected, and his honesty in providing an accurate reckoning had to be trusted by faith alone. Add to this that his delving into spiritualism flew in the face of church orthodoxy, and it wasn't long before suspicious parishioners began requesting a little chat about his accounting practices. When the reverend scorned the little chat option, formal charges dragged the matter to trial before the Iowa Presbytery. At the trial, Reverend Hummer characteristically lost his temper, stormed out of the room and declared the presbytery "a den of ecclesiastical thieves."

Meanwhile, the church building had advanced far enough by December 1846 that the basement could be used for worship. Probably this means that the floorboards of the main floor were in place to shelter under during a cold Sunday morning. While all the warm bodies huddled together might have made the chill bearable, imagine the cold sneers and nasty sideways frowns cast at Reverend Hummer as he led the service that morning. Hummer was entirely ignoring the authority of the Iowa Presbytery leadership and had been more brazen in his new beliefs about spiritualism. In the beginning of the new year, at the next session of the Iowa Presbytery, the leadership formally stripped Hummer of his rights and authority as a minister and expelled him from the Presbyterian Church. Hummer demanded that he was owed payment for his services to the church as both agent and minister. The Iowa Presbytery allowed him to take with him some moveable property and offered him $650 for his unpaid salary.

Hummer moved to Keokuk, setting up a new church aligned with a new Presbyterian sect called the New Lights. He soon put his funding expertise to good use raising money to build a church there. All it needed was a bell.

By 1848, the Iowa City Presbyterian Church was nearing completion. Its bell, the one purchased by Hummer, had already been installed in its belfry and was just awaiting the final carpentry details to enclose it inside. The belfry stood atop the gable at the front of the church. Here, the roof was supported by Doric columns framing the front porch with broad steps leading down to the street. Hummer, meanwhile, had never been paid his $650 from the Iowa Presbytery, and since he had paid for the bell out of his own pocket, he decided that the bell rightfully belonged to him. So one day late in the summer of 1848, Hummer and one of the trustees of his new church, Dr. J.W Margrave, quietly entered Iowa City aboard a wagon loaded with a stout rope and a block and tackle. At length, they came to the new Presbyterian church at Clinton and Market Streets. While Hummer climbed a construction ladder into the belfry, Dr. Margrave pulled the team away to allay suspicion and wait for the reverend's signal.

Up in the belfry, Hummer set up the block and tackle. Though the size of the bell is not known, according to a Meneely Bell catalogue, a twenty-seven-inch bronze bell alone can weigh about four hundred pounds. The block and tackle rig would have had to be adequate to get the bell free of its yoke and then swung over the side of the tower and past the gable by one man. Unfortunately for Hummer, once the bell tipped over the edge of the gable, he probably could not see where it was going to land.

The one thing a heist of any kind wants desperately to avoid is attention. Getting the bulky block and tackle carried up the ladder and into the belfry probably took quite a bit of time under the hot summer sun. Given Hummer's temper on a hot day, he probably was less than gentle with Margrave. Hummer's gambit doubtlessly attracted attention because by the time he had begun lowering the bell, a group of men had arrived with their own team and wagon. Seeing what was happening, they stealthily ordered Margrave to move his wagon out of the way and stay quiet or go swimming in the Iowa. Margrave obeyed while Eli Meyers swung his wagon into place and received the bell in the back of his wagon. When it was secured, he drove off, while another man, Anthony Cole, removed the ladder from the side of the building. Hummer was stranded in the belfry.

The activity in front of the church attracted a generous crowd from downtown. With Margrave prevented from helping by friends of the bell-nappers, Hummer beseeched the crowd for his ladder back. Of course, many in the crowd recognized the man on high and happily refused to help him. True to form, Hummer loosed his temper at the crowd below. In a fine fury, he hurled a steady stream of insults and profanities and even bricks and wooden planks. He vehemently cursed the congregation of the church, damning its building plus every member of the jeering throng below him. Hours passed, and when Eli Meyers's friends thought the wagon had been gone long enough, they let the doctor help Hummer down to solid ground. The two spent the rest of the day looking for the bell but did not find it. In a few days, the two men returned from Keokuk, bringing Dr. Margrave's daughter, a powerful medium, with them. Spirits, she said, told her the bell had been put down a well, so the two men commenced a random sampling of wells in the city to locate the bell. After failing to find it, Hummer returned to Keokuk.

Eli Meyers and a company of other men took the bell north to the confluence of the Iowa River and Rapid Creek. There, they sank the bell, but not before chaining it to the roots of an elm tree. The intention was to keep it submerged until the problem with Hummer blew over. It would have probably gone that way but for the lure of gold in California. In 1850, Eli Meyers and David Lamoreaux and a few others left Iowa City for California. Before they left town, though, they salvaged the bell, boxed it up and loaded it into a wagon. Because Lamoreaux was a Mormon, they intended to join a wagon train at Kanesville, Iowa, heading to Salt Lake City. Once there, they sold the bell to the Mormon tithing clerk for $600.

Hummer, however, did not give up on his bell. Through consultation with the spirit realm, he discovered that the bell had irrefutably been buried beneath the Old Capitol in Iowa City and was not jouncing in the back of a wagon bound for Salt Lake City. With little other recourse, he sued the Iowa Presbytery in 1853 for his $650 in lost wages. The court awarded him $450 but held him responsible for the bell's loss, so he got nothing.

The bell, meanwhile, stayed in its box for years (its clapper had been removed in Iowa City). There were efforts from Iowa City to retrieve it, but

Old Brick, Clinton and Market Streets. Do the shadows of a preacher's rage haunt this church because of a stolen bell?

these always seemed to run out of steam because no one from Iowa City could prove ownership. The last letter from Brigham Young in Salt Lake City to Charles Berryhill in Iowa City dates from April 1870, and he says, "I am still writing to let you know all that I can concerning it, and now if you are disposed to prove the property, pay charges, and take the bell away, I shall be very glad to have you do so, if not, you will do me a great kindness not to trouble me any more about it." A 1910 article in the collection of the Iowa Historical Society and a photo in a 1915 Old Settlers Association yearbook report the bell being in the Mormon Ladies Relic Chamber. In 1936, librarians in Des Moines and Salt Lake City launched a search for it, inquiring with the Daughters of the Utah Pioneers, the Mormon Church Historian's Office and the Latter Day Saints Bureau of Information, but no bell was found. The last inquiry from Iowa City came in 1998. Still, the bell has not been found.

Meanwhile, the church was eventually completed and dedicated in 1852. In 1856, a spark from a nearby carpenter's shop started a fire in the roof and burned it to the ground. Building began almost immediately on the site using some of the first church's remaining foundation. Old Brick arose, larger than the first church, and was finally completed in 1865. Its bell tower, meanwhile, featured a towering one-hundred-foot-tall spire holding a 2,874-pound bell. On June 20, 1877, the spire, bell and most of the front of the building were torn down by a tornado. The tower was replaced with the shorter crenellated tower that is still in existence today. (This is very similar to the Presbyterian church in West Point.)

EXCOMMUNICATION AND PRESERVATION

Old Brick served its congregation well into the late 1960s. As one of the oldest buildings in Iowa City, it was highly valued as a historic structure and a valuable part of Iowa City's heritage. But it was also old and drafty and sorely in need of repairs and updates. In 1967, First Presbyterian Church of Iowa City members voted 165 to 121 to demolish Old Brick and build a new church. Professor of English Joseph Baker and his wife, Tillie, opposed the motion because of the historical value of Old Brick. The couple wrote letters to the Presbyterian Synod, as well as publishing a controversial open letter in the *Iowa City Press-Citizen*. First Presbyterian's 14-member governing body, called the session, found that the Bakers were indiscreet in their passion to save the building and filed charges with the synod against the Bakers, saying their writings "were disruptive of the peace and unity of the church." In particular, the session charged that the Bakers had made derogatory statements about the pastors, the session itself, the building committee and other named persons. In response, the Bakers posted the session's charges against them on Old Brick's front door.

With the gauntlets thrown down, both sides dug in for a lengthy battle. The session declared that the Bakers had gone too far in expressing their dissent, while the Bakers asserted that it was within their rights to disagree with the church. The trial before the presbytery in Washington, Iowa, did something wholly unexpected: it excommunicated the Bakers. The Bakers appealed the state synod, which overturned the excommunication but continued the decision that the Bakers would be on indefinite suspension. The Bakers appealed to the National General Assembly, but it refused to hear the case.

For the building's sake, the Bakers' efforts attracted attention to Old Brick and other historic buildings but little else. In 1970, with the Bakers' case still slogging through the Presbyterian Church, their congregation decided against an architect's proposal for a new building at the site. Instead, they decided to put Old Brick up for sale.

In 1974, the University of Iowa bought Old Brick and prepared to tear it down to create a campus green space. While before only the Bakers and a few others had raised their voices to save the old church, half of Iowa City now mobilized against the university. After three years of public relations battles, the creation of numerous committees and fundraisers and the inevitable litigation, the building was purchased by the Old Brick Associates (which removed the pews to use the sanctuary as an auditorium). To guarantee the building's historic architectural integrity, it was placed on the National Registry of Historic Places, and a fifty-year preservation covenant was added to the deed. In 1987, it was sold to the Old Brick Episcopal Lutheran Corporation.

Does negative energy haunt Old Brick? Did Reverend Hummer's fiery curses against its congregation penetrate into the first church's foundation stones? Did his dabbling with mediums and spirits enable him to introduce a malevolent presence into the building site that periodically shakes the normal tranquility of its empty sanctuary with a vortex of anger and contention? Two witnesses who have worked there believe something hides and watches the old sanctuary late at night. Both have had experiences that left them wondering just what it is.

The first witness said that he was in the building after midnight. He was walking from the northwest doorway across the sanctuary. Typical of church architecture, there are three doors in the south wall of the sanctuary. These would have originally opened onto the aisles, with one in the center and one for each side aisle. In Old Brick, the one near the eastern wall is blocked, leaving only the doors in the center and near the west wall for use. The center door at the south side of the sanctuary stood about a third of the way open. The witness got about halfway across the room and was about twenty feet from the door when he noticed a shadow flit behind the door ahead. At just that moment, the door closed by itself. Wondering if someone else was in the building, he headed through the door near the west wall.

The doors open into a stairway that is beneath the bell tower. The stairway is wide open, and being over a century and a half old, it is also very noisy. The witness said he saw no one but heard noises that sounded like footsteps coming from the balcony above.

On a different evening, on a bitterly cold winter night, the other witness was alone and locking up the building after 10:00 p.m. He entered the sanctuary from the same door. The room was dark save for the hall light behind him. As he neared the south door, he heard a noise on the balcony above that sounded like footsteps. Like many churches, the balcony is open and mostly visible to the main floor. However, the witness could see no one. He passed through the south door onto the head of the stairway and into an uncomfortable pocket of cold air. Then he glimpsed the fleeting shadow of something moving swiftly up the balcony stairway on his left. Again, he heard what sounded like footsteps moving across the balcony above him. After only a few seconds, the noise stopped. The witness waited uneasily for a moment or two and then quickly decided that his curiosity could best be satisfied the next morning. When morning came, of course, there was nothing to be found, nor was anything missing.

Perhaps calmer minds not caught up in the moment would explain that old brick buildings contract on bitterly cold nights. Wooden beams creak and pop from the stress and make odd noises. Darting shadows could be from headlights of moving cars outside, and pockets of cold air happen in old drafty buildings on winter nights.

Maybe so, but wooden beams don't creak and pop in the cadence of a stride. Darting shadows from car headlights need to come through windows facing the street, and cold pockets of air don't usually form at the top of a stairway when the building's heating system is on. You can decide for yourself, of course. Old Brick currently operates as a nondenominational community center and hosts events ranging from wedding receptions to presidential candidate visits. The former sanctuary can be rented by anyone for almost anything…except maybe for debates.

BLACK'S GASLIGHT VILLAGE

*You undoubtedly did see a peacock…And if you had looked about you would have
seen many other strange and wonderful things, such as stained glass windows
and one apartment with a tree growing in the middle of it and even old and
fascinating tombstones all in a row outside in the yard.*
—*Ford Clark,* Cedar Rapids Gazette, *1979*

The Gaslight Village is located at 414, 418, 422 and 426 Brown Street
between Gilbert and Johnson Streets. Actor Gene Wilder lived
(briefly) one door to the west, and author Kurt Vonnegut lived one door
to the east. The brick house at 414 Brown Street is listed on the National
Register of Historic Places as the Charles Berryhill Mansion. Its builder,
Charles Berryhill, hailed from Harrisburg, Pennsylvania, and became a
land speculator and printer in Iowa City. Some of his landholdings included
the tract that would eventually become home to Herbert Hoover in West
Branch and a section of land south of Iowa City that ran on a line from the
Iowa River to a lone tree around which buffalo liked to stand. This became
the town of Lone Tree. His son, James, moved to Des Moines and was
elected to the state legislature for several terms. Charles Berryhill also wrote
to Brigham Young in Salt Lake City in 1870 about bringing back Hummer's
bell and then let the matter drop. He died on May 29, 1874.

By the mid-1960s, though, the address at 414, 418, 422 and 426 Brown
Street had a new name: Black's Gaslight Village. The name is contradictory
and creepy: "Black" and ""Gaslight" suggest opposites—darkness and

414 Brown Street, the Charles Berryhill House in the Gaslight Village.

light—existing in the same space. Yet, strictly speaking, the Gaslight Village isn't so much haunted but haunting. Part ramshackle dump, part architectural folk art, part intellectual asylum, the Gaslight Village has long been an enclave for talented, creative, artistic and poor University of Iowa students. Even before the Vonnegut workshop years, it functioned as the unofficial student residences for the world-famous Iowa Writers' Workshop. The premises feature four buildings that have expanded over the years, following an almost whimsical building code of their own. Walls were made entirely of doors, bowling balls and even footstones from a forgotten cemetery.

But along with the comedy and whimsy, the place has seen tragic illness, suicides, violence and fatal accidents. Almost as if they tumbled out of a Vonnegut novel, comedy and tragedy entwine here. For example, in the early hours of October 19, 2008, David Christian strangled his neighbor and drinking buddy, Michael Steward, after the two got into a fight over a game of chess. The *Daily Iowan* reported the Gaslight Village's reaction:

On Monday, friends and neighbors placed beer cans and other seemingly random items—a stick of butter, grapes—outside of [Michael] *Steward's apartment door, which was emblazoned with: DEAD. The word was written thickly in black ink. Underneath it, a knife was jammed into the door. Pinned to the wall was Steward's picture with "Tin Man is dead" and "mostly ghost" written on it.*

One of the myths surrounding the Gaslight Village is that the house was once a station on the Underground Railroad. Another is that it was originally the site of a graveyard. And yet another says the house was built as a real live train station. Historical records do not list the house as part of the Underground Railroad. Because those who violated the Fugitive Slave Act faced fines or prison, the stations on the Underground Railroad were kept secret. Yet since the house would have been along the route to another suspected station with strong Quaker ties, Terrell Mill, it is a possibility that the Berryhill Mansion may have been a rest stop. Since Charles Berryhill's son, James, was raised a Republican, the party that opposed slavery, this lesser role is worth considering. As for the graveyard, the only cemeteries in town are to the east. No one knows exactly where Henry Black got the footstones. It is possible they might even be a stonecutter's mistakes or rejects. Lastly, somewhere in his travels throughout eastern Iowa, Henry Black picked up a wooden railroad baggage cart that languished for years on the porch of the Berryhill house. Later, in the mid-1980s, it picked up a pot of geraniums and was moved into the sunshine. While numerous historic plat maps of Iowa City show a railroad going down the middle of Brown Street, the line was never built. The railroad ran out of money before it could be completed. A portion of that graded roadbed lies to the east in Hickory Hill Park.

Henry Black has been described as benignly cantankerous, a rugged individual, a slave driver, a slumlord and, in polite company, an ornery so-and-so. Born in 1902, he earned a master's degree in 1934 and briefly worked as a high school English teacher. Later, he switched to peddling the *Merriam-Webster Dictionary* to schools and other institutions throughout eastern Iowa. In 1943, he bought the large white house at 422 Brown Street and began raising a family with his first wife, Laura. In 1946, there was a shortage of housing in town, so the City of Iowa City asked Henry to rent rooms to GIs returning from service in World War II. Henry took this inch-long offer and ran twenty miles with it. Not only did he rent rooms to the GIs, but he also built onto his house, adding over fifty-three rooms, which he rented out to students. Next, he built another housing unit from salvaged materials in his backyard and allowed the students to trade their labor for rent (an offer he later advertised in the newspaper). He also had his two oldest sons working on additions, including a two-story barn that he called the Chalet. The city launched a legal action to stop him, citing too many apartments in one lot—and lost. Construction slammed onward. In the midst of this, though, Laura contracted cancer. She died at home in June 1954. Henry remarried a younger woman, and more children came into his life.

In 1960, Henry bought the Charles Berryhill Mansion next door, built additions on that and rented it out to poor graduate students studying the arts. The next year, he obtained a permit from the city to construct picnic shelters but instead built a twenty-five-unit apartment house. A group of fourteen Brown Street property owners tried to stop him, saying that he was building substandard housing and complaining that permits for buildings on the Brown property were obtained "under pretense that they were to be used for playhouses and other non-housing purposes." One of Henry's former residents defended his former landlord at the city council meeting, saying, "I have yet to live in apartments as nice as those. They are peculiar, but they are standard in every way." Eventually, a judge intervened and said he could keep the place as a rental if he had tenants living in each apartment within a few days. Henry advertised sleeping rooms for fifteen dollars a month in the local paper. The twenty-five rooms were filled in just two days in spite of the fact that no windows or doors had been installed in any of them.

Henry furnished his apartments with antique furniture, rugs and even books. In several apartments, entire walls of old books provided not only a diversion from student life but also insulation against the Iowa weather. What he couldn't use to furnish his rooms, he sold through the local paper. For years, antique oriental rugs, rare books and five-dollar bowling balls were advertised in the classifieds.

Both his older sons committed suicide in the early 1960s. It's rumored that sometime around then, the city became upset with the un-mowed grass at the village. Henry planted sunflowers, rose bushes and wildflowers. "Now make me mow!" he told the city inspectors.

In 1965, Kurt Vonnegut arrived in Iowa City to teach at the Iowa Writers' Workshop and set up house in the turreted Victorian mansion to the east of the Gaslight Village. The two years Vonnegut lived on the other side of the fence are still viewed fondly as the workshop's salad days (mostly because the people who were students then are now tenured legends themselves). Vonnegut and his wife, Jane, were known to step over the fence to visit and drink with his students. Henry and his special village were by that time a growing local legend, a totally open and free hippie art haven among his shrieking peahens, totem poles and house with a tree growing through it. Already in his sixties, Henry took to walking with an ivory-handled cane, which he insistently tapped on the apartment doors each month to demand the rent. Dread shivered through his tenants on those days because Henry was the devil wanting his due. Nevertheless, the writers, playwrights, actors and artists moved to the "folk art you could live in." By all accounts, Henry enjoyed both the bohemian atmosphere and battling city attorneys to keep the place open—even when it meant a lawsuit from his neighbor, Kurt Vonnegut, after Jane fell and injured her knee during a visit to a student's apartment during a summer pig roast.

Yet the same creative minds that can invent and spin wonder and joy can also chain themselves to depression. During the summer of 1965 or 1966, an undergrad writer had been up all night with a friend singing Beatles songs. Later on, the friend returned and found the young writer's body hanging from a rope in one of the basement apartments of the original Black residence. Sadly, it would not be the last.

Henry Black died in 1978. His wife, Frances, had scarcely time to leave the graveside before she had to fight city attorneys with a list of building code violations. They contended that improper ventilation, an insufficient number of toilets, inadequate fire escapes and other housing code violations made the complex uninhabitable. Nearly sixty Gaslight Village residents banded together to fight the city attorneys trying to condemn the village. Improvements and fire escapes were installed. Plumbing and electrical fixtures were brought into compliance. Then, to cap it off as an end-run around a window-dimension violation, the Charles Berryhill Mansion was named to the National Register of Historic Places—which forbade modernizing the noncompliant windows. Eventually, city inspectors got what compliance they needed, and the city council probably realized it could profit more from taxing the place than the hell it would raise by destroying it.

While the village was saved from the city, its rickety construction could not be saved from the ravages of Iowa's seasons. Time wore on the buildings. In the mid-1980s, they were constantly undergoing repairs, usually at the hands of Henry and Frances's sons. Finally, in 1987, Frances sold the village. The peahens stopped screaming in the wee hours. Black's was no longer Black's.

All the same, life at Black's continued in the same unique way. Even though the sensational Vonnegut party time had ended long before, the village had moved into a gentler, more civilized rhythm that was vastly out of sync with what had become the thumping beer party houses in the rest of town.

In 2005, a new owner acquired the Gaslight Village and made extensive renovations to the buildings. It now houses about seventy people, mostly students, in a civilized and respectful atmosphere that some have said is the ideal place to write a book. That said, tragedy still invades this artist colony: there was a suicide in 2004 and the murder in 2008. Perhaps Vonnegut summed up the artist's life at Black's best in one of his rules about writing: "Be a Sadist. No matter how sweet and innocent your leading characters, make awful things happen to them—in order that the reader may see what they are made of."

Are there ghosts at the Gaslight Village? Are there powerful psychic impressions of talented individuals who have lived there before causing strange phenomena? Possibly. But their spectral bumps and thumps may have mingled so long in the heaving and creaking of the ramshackle buildings that the spirits might have given up. Still, in all seriousness, some inmates tell stories of vivid glimpses of people who disappear. Other residents scoff and retort that these sightings really depend on what illegal substances the witnesses were concealing in their bloodstream at the time. Because old tenants move out and new ones arrive almost monthly, stories seldom corroborate. Yet only one tale continues to this day. During storms near the end of the month, as the raindrops smack onto the pavement outside, some tenants are sure they hear old Henry Black still tapping with his cane at their door for the rent.

E.C. MABIE THEATRE

Actors' theatres have a long tradition of being haunted. This includes the tradition of leaving the theatre closed one night a week, typically Mondays, to allow the ghosts to stage their own plays. Another one is that the lamp left on in the middle of the stage, called the "ghost lamp," is there so the ghosts can read their lines—although its day-to-day use is to deter living actors from walking across a darkened stage, falling to their deaths in the orchestra pit and joining that spectral troupe of players who refuse to pay their Actors' Equity Association dues.

The 457-seat E.C. Mabie Theatre on the University of Iowa campus is thought to have at least one ghost. Some years ago, a marketing director was working late in the theatre. He was certain that he was alone in the building and was busy in his office, which at the time was located directly under the audience seating section. Abruptly, he heard footsteps above him, moving gradually from one side to the other. Then, just as suddenly as they started, they stopped. The details, however, are not clear on whether it was a Monday night. In June 2008, the basement of the Theatre Building, including offices and the costume shop (nearly nine thousand square feet), was heavily damaged by flooding. In November, students cleaning a flood-damaged area that was once the costume shop witnessed a strange shadow linger before vanishing. As with most theatre ghosts, the spirit is well known and thought to be none other than the first director of the University Theatre Department, Edward Charles Mabie.

E.C. Mabie Theatre on the University of Iowa campus. Playwrights think the theatre school's first boss, who died in 1956, still wants to direct.

E.C. Mabie was born in Le Claire, Wisconsin, in 1892. He attended Dartmouth, earning both his bachelor's and master's in political science. Having finished his degrees in 1916, he married Grace Chase. The following year, he joined the faculty of Illinois Wesleyan College. In 1918, he taught English and speech at the University of Kentucky as an assistant professor. Mabie arrived in Iowa City about 1920 to begin teaching as an associate professor in the Department of Public Speaking. At that time, the department was headed by Glenn Merry and had a focus on debate. Because the university had no formal theatre organization, play productions were instead put on by the numerous university student clubs. About that time, the Englert Theater, founded by William Englert (son of brewer John Englert), had been used as a production venue. When the Englert increased its rental fees, eight clubs banded to become the University Theatre and chose Mabie to be its first director. Mabie's job was to secure a space for the group to stage productions. In little time, he struck a deal with the University of Iowa that if the administration provided the stage in MacBride Auditorium, as well as lights and curtains, he would ensure that all University Theatre productions would be performed there. Soon afterward, Mabie started a new graduate master's program in theatre and then launched a new theatrical group called the Out-of-Door Players. The group put on summer productions using outdoor spaces throughout the campus.

In 1923, the dean of the school, Professor Carl E. Seashore, and Merry were having a heated discussion about the public speaking degree program when the dean reportedly called the department "an art department that never should be allowed a doctoral degree in its own right." After much anguish and consideration, Merry resigned. In the wake, Mabie was elevated to acting head. The department rapidly went through a series of changes. In 1926, it was renamed the Department of Speech. By 1929, the university had created the School of Fine Arts. Mabie's department was christened the Department of Speech and Dramatic Arts.

In 1925, Mabie took over as department head (holding this post until he died in 1956). As head of the new Theatre Arts Department, he set about finding studio space for plays. He also instituted the importance of new plays, encouraging playwrights with their craft. Consequently, plays written and refined in Iowa traveled to New York City and were produced on Broadway. The fame of the school and its faculty spread.

In the 1930s, because of radio and talking motion pictures, the University Theatre group was the only company producing plays in Iowa City. While MacBride Auditorium sufficed as a theatrical space, its design better suited it to oratory or simple productions. The backstage area was tiny and the lighting space was confined, and these two traits limited the choice of plays for production. The administration began plans for developing a theatre space in the Iowa Memorial Student Union for a seven-hundred-plus-seat theater, but because of the financial problems of the Great Depression, the plans were shelved. Mabie's dream for a permanent space lingered in limbo indefinitely.

At last, an opportunity presented itself in 1933, when the university acquired land on the marshy west side of the Iowa River. Together with music chair Philip Greeley Clapp, President Walter Jessup and union director Rufus Fitzgerald, the four designed a riverside campus for the arts. Throughout 1934 and into 1935, Mabie scrambled for grants from the New Deal's Public Works Administration, the Civil Works Program and the Rockefeller Foundation. Even though there was a lot of work left unfinished (paint and plaster weren't applied in the auditorium until 1937), the theatre building was opened on November 7, 1936, with the premiere of E.P. Conkle's play *Two Hundred Were Chosen*, which was undergoing production simultaneously on Broadway.

As the engine that drove the university theatre department, Mabie possessed an unrelenting commitment to theatre. He ran the department in conditions that mirrored the professional theatre at that time. Almost like running a theatre boot camp, he made sure that every one of his students knew about every facet of theatre. They worked as actors, costumers, riggers, lighting techs and scenery carpenters, in addition to writing plays. Mabie changed degree requirements to include creative work to be accepted as a thesis and personally supervised students in the MFA program until his death.

He was also known to be a fierce-tempered autocrat. Both students and faculty called him "the Boss." His colleague, Harold Hansen, once remarked, when one of the secretaries told him the Boss wanted to see him after class, that he "went with some fear and trembling. A trip to the Boss's office was much like a trip to the woodshed at home."

In 1937, a young Thomas "Tennessee" Williams arrived at the University of Iowa to learn playwriting from Mabie. The student-teacher relationship had numerous rocky moments. The Boss was not only autocratic, but he was also an archconservative in his concept of theatre and had little tolerance for departures into experiment. Some of Williams's biographers have called Mabie's reaction to Williams as visceral, citing the time Mabie referred to him as "that pansy." Williams's work suffered a major setback during 1938 as he was wrapping up his bachelor of arts studies. As a student in Mabie's playwriting class, he was expected to read his plays aloud for the class. He had just finished reading his new play, *Spring Storm*, aloud to the class and was met with silence and embarrassment due to its highly sexual content. According to Williams, Mabie up and dismissed the seminar, saying, "Well, we all have to paint our nudes!"

With the growth of the broadcast industry through the 1930s and into the 1950s, Mabie began diversifying the theatre program into radio and then later television. At the same time, he constantly lobbied the university administration for funding to complete the theatre building.

In the early 1950s, Mabie suffered a series of strokes but fought his way back from each one to continue teaching. Then, in February 1956, at the age of sixty-four, he died of a heart attack after a full day of teaching. Twenty years later, his Dramatic Arts Building was renamed the E.C. Mabie Theatre.

So is it just actor superstition that Mabie roams the halls of his theatre? Some might argue that it probably is—if only because many of Tennessee Williams's plays, including *Spring Storm*, have been performed at the theatre building without incident. But the Boss was never one to let control slip easily from his hands while he was alive. Some of his last students would agree that he directs every aspect of the Monday night afterlife productions. It's even said that all kinds of havoc befall a production if his portrait in the theatre lobby is even slightly knocked askew. It's also known that the Boss has no compunction about barging into critique of the department's current efforts. Each year, student playwrights perch nervously in the audience to watch their own efforts produced during the annual Playwright's Festival. Many of them claim to see a shadow seated at the back of the theatre.

As each play ends, the figure shifts uneasily, and a low mutter can be heard that seemingly says, "They are all still painting nudes."

BLACK ANGEL

THE FELDWERT MONUMENT

On Sunday morning, November 5, 1922, Iowa City's families fired up coal furnaces to ward off the dank mid-autumn chill. The thick, black smoke drifted lazily northeastward over the Bohemian neighborhood called Goose Town, where a light frost had dusted children's abandoned jack-o'-lanterns. Cooling and sinking as it went, the smoke skirted St. Wenceslaus Church and then eerily flitted through Oakland Cemetery until it reached a gentle hollow in the hillside. There, with grim familiarity, it briefly embraced the figure of a tall, downcast angel. It then drifted away, taking with it the angel's last tiny golden glint from the very top of her head.

The next morning, the cramped headline atop the second page of the *Iowa City Press-Citizen* proclaimed the news: "Black Angel in Cemetery." Truth be told, she had been growing blacker and blacker for years. So, too, were the stories and weird tales of why. The newspaper that morning said the angel had arrived in Iowa City that way—or at least it had been a dark color—but promised "the dark covering will duly be abraded or eroded by wind and water and sunlight" until it shines anew.

It's been one hundred years since she came to town, and she is still as black as can be—perhaps even fuliginous—and it's said that anyone who touches her dies in seven years.

The Black Angel—or the Feldwert Monument, as it is formally known—has been Iowa City's alter ego for a century. At nine and a half feet tall, the statue looms atop a granite pedestal a little over three feet high. The figure

"By daylight, grotesque and menacing,
by moonlight, weird and uncanny
—altogether out of keeping with its surroundings,
'The Black Angel' silently
guards the grave of some unknown person."
—Mildred Augustine, 1924

mournfully looks downward, its wings drooping, its arms stretched wide in a gesture suggesting somber surprise and warning. On the ground before it lies a level, unadorned concrete slab. The inscription on the front of the pedestal reads:

> RODINA FELDEVERTOVA
> Nicholas Feldwert 1825–1911
> Theresa Feldwert 1836–

Part enigma, part legend and part focus of adolescent fright rites, Oakland Cemetery's famous sculpture draws hundreds of visitors yearly. Some come to study the angel as a work of a Czech-American master sculptor. Some come to see an icon of Iowa City's popular culture and literary heritage. Some come just to stand before its frightful form. But all are filled with a rush of questions begging for answers: Who were these people? Who made the statue? Where did it come from? What is this bizarre inscription on the side? What's the tree stump thing next to it? Why is it black?

Of course, there are other visitors who come only at midnight. They come to tempt fate and learn if the stories are really true.

One spring, a pregnant woman walked under the Angel's outstretched wing and later miscarried. In the fall of 1918, a healthy young man who was strolling past it with his sweetheart leapt onto the pedestal in a moment of high spirits and kissed the statue. He soon took sick with the flu and died. A known adventuress supposedly had an illicit evening rendezvous at the very foot of the Angel and died on the spot of heart failure. Fraternity initiates were compelled to practice all sorts of strange rites there in the fall. On Halloween, families living on North Governor Street across from the burial ground locked their doors because they saw strange glows and heard weird murmurs coming from just over the hill from that part of the cemetery. As fathers kept watch at the front parlor window, mothers warned their children to never—for the sake of their immortal souls—venture among the wizened stones in Oakland Cemetery on Halloween night while the Black Angel was abroad.

Strange rumors about the Black Angel had been popular knowledge well before the tantalizing first few were printed in the *Press-Citizen* in 1922. Stored for several months after arriving in November 1912, the statue was erected in Oakland Cemetery in 1913 and blackened so quickly that it naturally led some sensitive folks to suspect that a horrible curse or unnatural forces stalked among the tombs on the hill. Weird stories about why it was black emerged from "reliable sources." Mildred Augustine, a University of Iowa sophomore living in Currier Hall, set out to investigate these stories. Later in her life as author Carolyn Keene, she would write the first twenty-three Nancy Drew mysteries. Her exposé on the cause of the Angel's blackness might have loosed more fiction than facts. It was published in the *Iowa Magazine*, with excerpts appearing in the *Press-Citizen* on September 2, 1924.

One story she records tells how the Angel was erected by a wealthy Bohemian woman in memory of a son who fell in France during the First World War. The Angel was supposedly bought in Europe and changed from pure white marble to jet black because of the sea air during the voyage. Another story she quotes says the statue changed color on the day the soldier was buried. Yet another says the angel was white until it was struck by lightning.

Augustine goes on to explain that the statue was, in fact, bought as a monument for Theresa Feldwert's first husband and a son who died in childbirth. She points out that it was bought from a traveling salesman and was contracted to be carved from imported white marble that cost half of Theresa's life savings. Yet when it was delivered, it was a crude piece "roughly cast out of an inexpensive metal—apparently iron." Since Theresa was out of state at the time, Augustine asserts, she had no way of knowing "that she had been hopelessly swindled in her purchase." Unfortunately, Augustine's facts here are dead wrong.

Still, Augustine's factual problems may hint at her own fear of the dreadful figure. (Oddly enough, the one-line filler item that follows her excerpted article in the *Press-Citizen* ominously reads: "Most suicides occur in mid summer." A synchronistic warning, perhaps?) Had the Angel been made of iron and painted black, its appearance would be even more sensational, for there would be slender trails of rust running down its sides resembling dried blood. Without a doubt, Augustine saw the statue (perhaps only in a photo), but from her mistaken assessment it sounds as if she avoided getting near it. In spite of her efforts, Augustine's investigation succeeded in adding more to the Black Angel's lore. Stories and details merged, multiplied and spun themselves into spooky tales of sin and shame.

TALES OF SIN AND SHAME

Penora Stuart leaned languidly in her negligee against her bedroom door rereading the telegram from her husband. "9 feet white marble angel [STOP] Ship Sept 17 Napoli [STOP] Arr Pt Reading NJ Oct 19 [STOP] Arr Iowa City Oct 31 [STOP] Love Leo [STOP]."

Penora sighed and then rubbed the new wedding ring on her finger as if it were a deep, aching bruise. She had meant that he should send her a marble angel as a joke. "I'll be more faithful than a marble angel!" she told him on the platform as he boarded the train. Now he was sending her a nine-foot-tall statue?

"Idiot!" she snarled, putting her face in her hand. No, make that immensely talented idiot and very soon acclaimed and rich idiot, she corrected herself. Still. *Nine feet tall?*

The sharp snore erupted from her bedroom with all the fury of a walrus's love cry. Penora burst into a silvery laugh. She set the telegram on the little table by the door and rushed back to the bedroom. Her lover, Kent, had

Did infidelity or murder turn her black? Only when a maiden, pure and innocent of the world and men, receives her first kiss will she return to white.

kicked off the covers in his sleep and now stretched across the bed like a horizontal version of Michelangelo's David.

I just love great art, she giggled to herself. She bent down and kissed his ankle and then impetuously continued kissing up his leg until...

"Bring 'er about smartly, Mr. Jarvik!" Thunder banged and rolled above them. Captain Olson had to shout the order across the bridge to the helmsman.

"Aye, aye, sir!" Jarvik answered, hauling hard on the wheel. The freighter heaved over smoothly at first, but as it passed over a swell, it wallowed.

"Damn it!" Olson yelled as he watched the long line of crated autos shift on the fore deck. "Keep 'er even, Mr. Jarvik, or we'll dump these fine motor cars in the drink!" He blew into the speaking tube that wound down to the engine room, "Speed now, if you please, Mr. Holt!"

At once, there came a sickening thud from the fore deck as the cargo derrick collapsed onto a particularly tall and wide crate lashed to the end of the crated Bugattis. There in the wreckage, both Jarvik and Olson saw a hint of a gleaming white head and broad white wings. Suddenly, lightning flashed, striking the big broken crate. Both men shut their eyes, turning their heads away as thunder tore the sky overhead. When they opened their eyes, what remained of the derrick and most of the crates was blackened and fitfully burning in the rain.

Seven months later, Penora stepped into the dim railroad freight house and made her way around small crates and packing cases toward the spot where the statue had been stored. Barely lit at the far end of the freight house by a single lantern set upon a packing case, she saw her husband's familiar form tugging at large canvas tarp. "Is that you, Leo? The station master phoned," she called.

"Penora, darling!" Leo called back. "I'm sorry I didn't come to the house first, but I wanted to come check on the statue. Bizarre letter from the railroad agent at Port Reading."

She nervously positioned herself behind the broad packing case with the lantern. A few feet in front of her, she could see her fiancé tugging at the tarp and caught the stink of charred wood. "Is that the crate?" she asked. "The freight agent told me only the crate had been damaged. Is it all right?"

"The ship was struck by lightning. Oh, I wish they hadn't stored this on its side." Leo tugged at the tarp. Suddenly it tore, and he fell, crashing into crate slats. He got to his feet but leaned to one side in an awkward stance. "Damn. I've got myself stuck."

"Are you all right?" Penora asked, becoming worried. She had agreed to come meet him and had decided to concoct some tale to gain his sympathy for her condition. Yet here in the shadows, she was having trouble thinking of something, and she began losing her nerve.

"I'm fine, just got my leg tangled in this blasted tarp. I just can't see anything back here," he complained. "Could you bring that lantern around?"

"Um, is it safe to walk back there?"

"Perfectly. Just go around the end there and along the wall."

"Maybe I should go get the boy out front," she stalled.

"Don't be silly. Just bring the light around and I can get out of here."

Penora gathered her wits and her will and picked up the lantern. Her mind raced as she made her way around the crates. As she came along the wall toward Leo, she struck upon the idea of holding the lamp high enough to obscure her body with shadow from the lamp's bottom.

Leo, meanwhile, busied himself with pulling aside crate slats. "Well, it doesn't seem she's been broken. Not even a chip," he said, reaching his hand inside the crate. "I wonder why he said 'spoiled'?"

As Penora drew near him, he heaved aside the crate's lid. Instead of the gleaming pure white angel that should have reposed inside, the two beheld an angel that was thoroughly black.

"Impossible," Leo muttered. "I carved this for you! I chose the block myself! Not even the slightest stain or imperfection. Pure…"

Penora suddenly felt sick with guilt. "When was the storm?"

Leo looked at her incredulously. "The letter said September 20."

At that, Penora burst into loud sobbing and would have dropped the lamp, but Leo snatched it from her hand and in the movement caught sight of her belly. He froze, stammering.

A relative said that Leo left town soon after. When Penora's time came, she delivered a son, but it was stillborn. When Leo heard the news, he sent money to have the angel moved from storage and placed on the child's grave.

In June 1912, Professor Brooks Nodaway took his new bride, Cambria Humseton, on a honeymoon to tour Athens, Greece. Since Professor Nodaway studied ancient Greek history, he and his wife spent hours in museums and the Parthenon. They also visited the mountain town of Penteli, where the marble for the Parthenon was quarried. Both husband and wife were amazed with its quality. It was fine stone, almost pure white that in full sun gave off an almost golden sheen.

Barely had their visit begun when Cambria started complaining of exhaustion, and soon she was unable to leave her bed. The couple sought out doctors and soon learned from a heart specialist that her condition was deteriorating. The day she died, Cambria made Brooks promise he would bring her body back to Iowa City and, on her tomb, place a marble statue of an angel made from the lovely Penteli marble they both loved so much. Brooks promised it would be done.

But because she was so young and so much in love, she demanded one more thing from her husband. "I am so worried that when I pass on, you will forget me," she said weakly.

Brooks shook his head.

"I want you to swear you will love me forever and that you will never be unfaithful to me," she went on, her voice trailing off.

The professor, who was beside himself with grief, could only croak, "I swear, my dearest."

"So you say, my love," she gasped, her breathing more labored. "But I shall know by my tombstone's color if you stray." With that, she died.

A few weeks later, the funeral was over. The new husband found himself alone as a new widower. Being a man of considerable energies, he put himself to work securing the monument he had promised. Within six months, it arrived in Iowa City and caused a sensation when it was set on its pedestal over his wife's grave. On sunny days, he would walk to the grave to behold it gleaming in the sun.

One sunny mid-September day during his walk to the grave, he met an attractive younger woman who had set up an easel and was sketching the statue. He asked her casually if she liked the statue.

"I think it's very modern, but it is certainly reminiscent of classical Greek entablature, and the hue seems very like the Penteli marble I saw at the Parthenon when I was a girl," she answered.

Brooks mastered his delight just long enough to sputter, "Really?"

Her name was Aurora Stanley. They talked for more than an hour, and at the end, she accepted his invitation to dinner.

In the weeks afterward, he found himself spending more and more time with Aurora and visited the grave less and less. As October wore on, the sextons in Oakland Cemetery noticed that the Angel's sheen seemed to be fading each day.

In the morning on November 1, the sextons found the angel had turned completely black.

At precisely twenty-seven minutes past 11:00 p.m. on the night of April 30, 1909, Pastor Randolph Imogen Magnolia rose from his knees greatly distressed. He steadied himself by lightly touching his hand to the wall for just a moment and took a deep breath.

A terrible tragedy, he counseled himself. You have done nothing wrong, you merely defended yourself. It was the work of one of those ruffians he runs with—yes, they were after his money. They did this foul deed to this wretched boy.

He took a deep breath again and then picked up the cushion from where he left it, pressed hard onto the now dead, blue-lipped face of his teenage son, Nicholas.

Act! he muttered to himself. Taking the cushion with him, he raced into the basement of the house and there doused it with plenty of kerosene before setting it alight in the furnace. Next, he ran to the telephone and called Dr. Plano, a member of his congregation. After that, he called the police and told them a gang of young tuffs had broken in and he feared his son was dead. When he hung up, he looked wildly around the room. He needed an injury. Something bloody but not drastic. A scalp wound, yes. Now what would serve? Ah, the gilded mirror in the hallway. Yes, it had been a wedding gift from one of his dratted late wife's relations, but he never particularly liked it.

With no further adieu, he bent down his head and ran full speed into the mirror. Glass flew everywhere. He rolled on the floor dazed for a moment, wondering if his stunt had worked. His head hurt badly enough. He lurched to his feet, and as he stood up a torrent of blood streamed past his eyes onto the floor. Perfect!

All he had to do now was collapse near the phone and wait and remember to keep his head. Oh, they would believe him, he reassured himself. After all, he was a man of God.

In due course, Randolph's congregation rallied around to support him. Such a tragedy, such a burden, the church ladies muttered behind him. That made him secretly smile. He made a show of carrying on heroically and displayed the occasional weak moment judiciously. At his son's funeral, one of his colleagues from a nearby church performed the service for him. Randolph considered this a great favor, for deep inside, he had despised the troublesome, spoiled brat and sincerely doubted his skill at finding a nice thing to say over his grave. The lad was finally laid to rest with many tears in Oakland Cemetery.

The police, meanwhile, had no problem rounding up some of the usual suspects. Pastor Randolph pointed out two as culprits, purely because he didn't like the shapes of their noses. Both youths had prior records, so the trial and the verdict were only formalities. Within a week, the two were breaking rocks in Fort Madison.

Pastor Randolph, meanwhile, settled down to plan how he would enjoy the annuity he received, instead of his son, from his late wife's estate.

When his own son turned fourteen, Dr. Plano decided that the boy no longer required the discipline of a military academy and brought him home to attend City High. Pastor Randolph had not seen the boy since he was seven. After church services one Sunday morning, as the pastor busily exchanged greetings, smiles and handshakes with his congregation, a young man approached him, holding out his hand. When Randolph clasped the lad's hand, something of an electric wave pulsed through him, for the boy was the splitting image of his own dead son.

"Good morning, sir," the boy said in a confident, clear voice.

Pastor Randolph spluttered, not sure if he was seeing a ghost. He blinked several times.

"Pastor Randolph," Dr. Plano smiled, putting his hand on the boy's shoulder. "This is my son Seymour."

"Good Lord!" Randolph exclaimed, though more in relief than surprise.

The trio made small talk for a few moments, and the father and son moved on. Later, though, Pastor Randolph sat alone in his study haunted by the sight of the young man.

It can't be, he told himself. But it is, he's alive. *Don't be ridiculous. He's dead. That terrible tragedy, remember*. No, it WAS him. *He's dead.* I know what I saw. *For the last time, HE'S DEAD!*

From then on, Sundays for Pastor Randolph were never the same. Seymour Plano always sat in the same seat, third row on the center aisle, and paid rapt attention to his every word. Pastor Randolph found it so difficult to pay attention that he began reading his sermons to the congregation and avoided making eye contact as much as possible. Afterward, Seymour would wait to be the last one in line to discuss some fine point of his sermon with him. Randolph would put a small effort to endure the boy for a few minutes but would always squirm loose as quickly as he could. Sundays in his study soon became a living hell.

It's him, he told himself, brooding at his desk. Why can't you be sensible? *You know it's him—he has taken over Seymour.* Shut up. *He wants revenge.* He's dead, this is a different kid, now shut up. *No, you killed him for the money—pay him somehow or they'll find out.* Stop it, just stop it! *You won't turn yourself in but you must pay for your crime.* HE'S DEAD—SHUT UP! *Never—not until you pay…*

Finally, after several sleepless nights in a row, Pastor Randolph determined that he could atone for his misdeed by commissioning a bigger tombstone for his son's grave. If he could somehow placate his son's spirit and his own conscience, then he would have some peace at last. He used his contacts with the university to locate a source of pure white marble from Colorado and then located a sculptor in Chicago to carve the angel. It cost him half of what was left of the annuity money, nearly $7,000, but in just two months, the work was done. The Angel was delivered to Iowa City via rail and then transported by wagon and eight-hitch team of draft horses to bring it to Oakland Cemetery. It was erected three years to the date of his son's death, on April 30, 1912—*Walpurgisnacht*, the night of the witches.

No one thought anything of the violent thunderstorm that blew into town that night. There was so much lightning that many people in town claimed they could read by it. On May Day morn, the sextons at Oakland Cemetery went about their business, clearing away some fallen branches, until they came to the crest of the hill and saw the Angel at the boy's grave. Stunned and speechless, they sent a boy to fetch Pastor Randolph as quickly as he could come.

When Randolph got to the cemetery, they say he took one look, fell to his knees, clasped his hands together and screamed out his confession to the murder.

Because the Angel had turned completely black.

For years, the older folks in town whispered that after his hanging, both heaven and hell refused to claim his soul. So to this day, it floats suspended in that spectral limbo seen only by the Black Angel.

To Dr. Kent Clearfield, Clarinda Hepburn was absolutely the perfect bride. Tall but demure, pretty, intelligent but deferential on financial matters, she possessed those exquisite faculties required for furnishing and managing a fine Summit Street house. That she seldom spoke of her family puzzled him, though some generous Chicago uncle of some sort did provide her with a substantial income and this assuaged any qualms he might have over the quality of her character. Plus, there was the added bonus of no foreseeable contention with a mother-in-law. The night she said yes to his proposal of marriage, he felt so elated that he practically wept himself to sleep from sheer joy.

For several years, they were very happy together. Patients and lectures at the University Hospital dominated the doctor's time but spread his reputation and began building him a promising career. Clarinda, meanwhile, belonged to a local Christian ladies' temperance league, which kept her very busy and earned her much esteem and respect. Twice a month she would take the train to Chicago to visit her uncle, and once in a while she journeyed to St. Louis to visit a sickly cousin.

On a hot summer day in 1910, the railroad track roasting in the sun just west of Tipton warped enough to pull the spikes out of the track ties. The noon eastbound train from Iowa City hit the spot doing forty miles per hour, throwing the locomotive and its three cars down the embankment. Fortunately, all but one of the twenty-five passengers escaped injury. Unfortunately, the injured person was Clarinda. She died in the hospital that night, her devoted husband at her side.

Inconsolable for weeks over his loss, Dr. Clearfield eventually decided to erect a suitable monument to the ideals of devotion, dedication, beauty and loyalty that were epitomized in his beloved wife. Clarinda's local temperance league friends encouraged him and promised they would celebrate her life and noble work for the cause with a special church service in her honor. The finest close-grained, purest white marble was imported from Italy. For two years, a Chicago sculptor labored over the block until at last he finished the piece. It was brought to Iowa City and erected on her grave on October 31 with an immense canvas over it. The statue would be unveiled the next morning during a special All Saints Day service sponsored by the Woman's Christian Temperance Union.

On November 1, in the middle of the service, Dr. Clearfield pulled the rope to drop the canvas sheet from around the statue. When it fell, the crowd uttered a gasp of amazement. The statue had turned completely and utterly black as sin.

In the next few days, word of the statue spread. Before too long, an anonymous letter arrived from Chicago. In it, Dr. Clearfield discovered to his horror that his perfect wife did not have a generous uncle in Chicago. She had been, in fact, a highly paid courtesan much desired by the city's powerful and wealthy. She had used her life in Iowa to shield herself from certain troublesome clients.

It is said that the statue will once again turn white only when a maiden, pure and innocent of the world and men, receives her first kiss—one of betrothal—beneath the Angel's watchful eyes.

THERESA DOLEZAL FELDWERT

There are other stories that say Theresa Feldwert was an unusual, lonely woman who was an evil witch, so the angel on her grave turned black. There are others that say she was unfaithful or that she killed her infant son. The truth is an altogether different story.

Theresa Karásek was born October 14, 1836, in the village of Strmilov, Bohemia, which lies in the south central region of the modern Czech Republic. Her family was Catholic, and her father had served in the Austrian army. She was the youngest of four children; she had a brother and two sisters.

In April 1866, her mother died of uterine cancer, so it might be safe to say that Theresa spent months caring for her while she was sick. On November 27 of that year, thirty-year-old Theresa married Dr. František Doležal. A short time later, her new husband moved to Vienna, where he worked as a surgeon. Theresa stayed behind in Strmilov and gave birth to her first child, Otto, on February 2, 1868. The baby did not fare well and died two weeks later from "infantile convulsions."

In the wake of this tragedy, Theresa moved to Vienna to join her husband. There, she enrolled in the University of Vienna's Clinic of Obstetrics to train as a midwife. After earning her credentials, she returned to Strmilov.

Theresa Doležal Feldwert (1836–1924). *Photo provided by Timothy C. Parrot.*

It is there that her second son, Edward, was born on March 10, 1873. Her husband's fate, meanwhile, is not too clear. His practice being in Vienna, he lived apart from his wife and son. He would have been in his mid-fifties at the time, and it is possible he may have left her or died.

Interestingly enough, in 1877, Theresa secretly left her beloved Strmilov in the middle of the night, taking four-year-old Edward with her. She and her son reached the German port of Bremen and sailed for the United States. Once there, they headed westward until reaching the tiny Bohemian enclave in Iowa City in an area known as Goose Town. By March

716 East Bloomington Street. Edward Doležal died here in 1891.

1878, Theresa had begun advertising her services as a midwife in the *Slovan Americký*, a Czech newspaper read by many immigrants in the Iowa City and Cedar Rapids area.

By 1878, Theresa had been successful enough to buy her own home at 716 East Bloomington Street. In the spring of 1881, she installed a steam boiler system in the basement below the east room of her house. This she converted to a steam bath and advertised morning and evening Russian steam baths in the local newspapers.

During this time, both city directories and census records inaccurately listed her as a "Doctor." However, given the lack of state control over the medical profession at the time, this seems to have been a common occurrence. While Theresa obviously lacked the educational requirements, the State of Iowa did not formally establish regulations for medical practice until 1886. Until that time, nearly anyone could hang out a shingle as a doctor and perform surgeries, prescribe drugs and determine sanity without a license.

This was also the era of patent medicines. In Iowa, registered pharmacies were allowed to concoct their own lines of drugs and tinctures, most of which were liberally lubricated with alcohol. Pharmacists were also permitted to continue selling medicinal liquor when prohibition was instituted in 1884.

Theresa's beloved son, Eddie, took an interest in pharmacy work. He began working at Boerner Bros. Drugstore at 113 East Washington Street and had the intention of entering the University of Iowa to take up the study. However, just two months before turning eighteen, on January 9, 1891, he fell ill at work. Taken home to Bloomington Street, he steadily worsened until he died on January 14, 1891, of tubercular spinal meningitis.

Eddie's funeral was held at St. Mary's Catholic Church a few days later. His original grave in Oakland Cemetery is an underground crypt located on the east half of Lot 4 in Block 9. It is partially concealed behind a large sign a few yards east of the main office and adjacent to the entrance road. Although the grave is now empty, the original inscription still appears on the concrete slab. The crypt itself was accessible by opening a full-size metal door and then descending a stairway, but this feature has long since been filled in. The well-known six-foot-tall concrete sculpture of a tree trunk near the Black Angel was also part of the crypt setting. The highly detailed sculpture (complete with shelf fungus) was a common thematic device during Victorian times to indicate a life cut short. Several other smaller (and equally tragic) examples can be found in Oakland.

While it seems that Theresa tried to bury herself in her business, she still grieved bitterly over the loss of her son. In September 1891, Theresa announced in the *Slovan Americký* that she would be traveling to St. Paul, Minnesota, for a period of six months. A vacation might have seemed therapeutic at this point in her life. At age fifty-five, she had left her homeland under unknown circumstances, lost her first marriage and lost two children—Eddie being the one with whom she had bonded so closely. Now she was utterly alone, feeling angry, abandoned and vulnerable.

Her trip to St. Paul only complicated her life. While there, she met and married Joeseph Picha, a clothier who was also a Bohemian immigrant. By July 1893, the Pichas had sold the house on Bloomington Street and purchased a house at 332 North Johnson Street in Iowa City. Theresa soon took up midwifery again, but at about that time, her marriage fell apart.

Above, left: Edward Doležal's first tomb, Oakland Cemetery.

Above, right: Edward Doležal's tree-trunk monument, Oakland Cemetery.

Emotionally wounded again, Theresa fled to Chicago. There, she briefly owned and operated a laundry before returning to Iowa City for only two years. In July 1896, she traveled to Boston, Massachusetts, intending to stay for some months, but within the year, she had traveled to Eugene, Oregon. By March 1897, at the age of sixty, she was married again.

All of this moving around suggests that two sets of characteristics made up Theresa's character. One set is that she was energetic, independent minded and determined. The other is that she tended to react impulsively and dealt with emotionally challenging situations by avoidance. This period from 1891 to 1897 put her through so much grief and loss that her avoidance behavior (evidenced by her need to travel) may have exacerbated her problems making and maintaining personal attachments. She was hurt, emotionally confused and listless.

The man she married in 1897, though, seems to have been the right guy at the time. Born in 1825 in the village of Verl in West Phalia, Germany, Nicholas Feldwert had immigrated to the United States in 1850 and gradually made his way westward. In 1856, he fought in the Rogue River Indian War as a private in Company B, Second Regiment, Oregon

Mounted Volunteers. When they married, he was a seventy-two-year-old rancher who had been widowed twice. Here, perhaps, Theresa had found a kindred soul.

Misfortune then struck in the form of a rattlesnake. Theresa had been helping Nicholas make hay when she was bitten in the leg by a rattler. The potent venom is necrotic. A bitten adult limb can quickly whither, and the venom can progress into paralysis and death. In order to save her life, her lower leg was amputated. She would be confined to a wheelchair for the rest of her days.

In 1901, the Feldwerts signed a promissory note for $215 with a Dr. Meyers, who had promised to treat Theresa for an undisclosed ailment. Myers spoke German, and the Feldwerts felt they could trust a fellow countryman. When Meyers failed to provide any treatment, the Feldwerts refused to pay. Meyers, however, had sold the note to another party. This landed the Feldwerts in litigation that eventually wound its way to the Oregon Supreme Court. The Feldwerts complained that Meyers had misrepresented his services in the original note, and both testified that they could not read English. The note was written in English, and in it Meyers did not stipulate the services he was to provide, nor was he licensed to practice medicine in Lane County, Oregon. The court found that the Feldwerts could read English well enough to learn the nature of the contract and so found them to be negligent. Losing this case would resonate with Theresa in the future.

The following year, Nicholas Feldwert filed a claim for an Indian war pension for his service from 1855 to 1856. He was compensated for ninety-seven days of service at $2 per day. Less the $50 he had already been paid, the total amounted to $144, a tidy sum for the time.

Nicholas Feldwert died on January 19, 1911, of apoplexy (possibly a stroke) at the couple's home in Eugene. His body was cremated, and Theresa purportedly kept his ashes in a cigar box on a shelf in her kitchen. An administrator took over settling the estate because Theresa was described as not being able to care for herself. The administrator stated to the court that she was "crippled and enfeebled in health generally, and further having had one of her legs amputated below the knee, all of which renders said widow almost helpless." When the estate was settled, she inherited $19,513.45. In today's money, that would amount to almost $1 million.

It appears that Theresa had begun considering a new monument for her son, Eddie, sometime prior to Nicholas's death. By January 1911, she had already been in contact with her close friend and well-known Chicago-based Czech language publisher August Geringer to help find a suitable artist who would undertake the job. Geringer recommended Mario Korbel, a new talent whose work was just beginning to grab the fine art spotlight.

Mario Korbel was born in Bohemia. His father, Josef Korbel, was a Protestant, but his mother, Katherine—whose maiden name, coincidentally, was Dolezal—was Catholic. Immigrating at only age eighteen to New York and then Chicago in 1900, he took a job modeling ornamental interior moldings. In 1905, he returned to Europe to study art at the Royal Academy of Fine Arts in Munich and then moved on to attend the Académie Julian in Paris. He returned to Chicago in 1910 and began accepting commissions to sculpt both public and private works. He worked mostly in bronze and experimented with a variety of patina finishes. His works still fetch hefty sums at the famous Christie's auction house.

Theresa's plan for the new memorial was a sculpture that included a bronze version of the tree trunk monument at Eddie's grave. The contract Theresa signed with Korbel stated that the memorial was to follow her specifications, except that Korbel's artistic changes would be considered if Geringer, acting as her agent in Chicago, approved them. The terms were $2,500 up front and the other half upon completion. Korbel worked on the figure from January through May 1911. News of the memorial was reported in the *Press-Citizen* on March 20, 1912, saying that Korbel's model of the Angel had been "attracting a deal of attention at the Art Institute of Chicago." Harriet Monroe, art critic for the *Chicago Tribune*, sniped that it "fails of angelic quality" but added that it was "a soulful modern lady with wings."

The design did not pass muster with Theresa because it did not incorporate the tree trunk monument as per her original design. She initially refused to pay the remaining $2,500. Because Geringer, acting as her agent, had OK'd the change, she learned that she had no legal standing and so acquiesced to paying the balance.

The statue was cast by the Florentine Brotherhood Foundry in Chicago and thence shipped by rail to Iowa City in late 1912. It was very probably stored out of the elements over the winter while a suitable granite block could be quarried.

In 1913, Theresa returned to Iowa City. She sold her old home on North Johnson Street and for a while stayed with James Prybil, street commissioner for Iowa City. At seventy-six years old, she had begun to consider how to dispose of her fortune after her death. She had some negotiations with the mayor about statues, fountains, walkways, etc. for City Park, but this came to naught in the end. In August, she bought a home at 531 Center Street just south of Oakland Cemetery. In late autumn, a block of Barre granite was imported from Vermont, and the gleaming, golden Angel was mounted on top. Eddie's tree trunk monument was moved to its current position just under the Angel's gaze, and his body was placed in the vault at her feet. Nicholas's ashes were interred there as well.

That completed, an inscription was added on the south face of the block. Probably executed by a workman unfamiliar with Czech, the lines appear to be a poem composed by Theresa herself:

> For me, the clouds concealed the sun. the path was thorny;
> The days of my life passed without solace.
> You always accomplished your work only for the good of the world.
> You fold your arms, your head bows down, your spirit flies away into the distance,
> Where, after your suffering, an eternal reward awaits you.

The winter of 1913–14 was reportedly mild, with only one bitterly cold patch in February. A mild, wet winter combined with houses burning high-sulfur bituminous coal to the west of the cemetery doubtless created highly acidic conditions for the statue. Whereas most bronze statues turn a lovely tan-brown color, sometimes tinged with green, the sulfur dioxide in the air turned the Angel black in a very short period of time. Theresa was disappointed, having preferred the gold, but Korbel maintained that a shiny bronze statue in a cemetery was a "foolish monument." Even so, the story is told that Mrs. Magnolia Zetek, resident of 704 Reno Street since 1905, sometimes witnessed a pathetic sight. She would see Theresa wheel herself up the slope to the base of the Angel. There, she would pull herself up from her wheelchair, and then "Mrs. Feldwert used a knife to scrape at the statue to determine the reason for its blackness."

Theresa stayed on Center Street until the following May, when her weak condition forced her to move in with Josephine Nosek at 1020 Market Street. The Angel statue completed, her thoughts turned to her homeland, Strmilov. She had already sent to her hometown a third of her inheritance from her husband's estate, $6,400, which was eventually put toward building a poorhouse. Today, the building is a kindergarten educating children three to six years old, and the original plaque inset with her photo remains. By May 1916, Theresa had moved from Iowa City back to Eugene. For the next several years, she would continue to send money, letters and poems to Strmilov. These funds were distributed among its poor, used to buy a movie projector and put toward building a gymnasium.

It had been her intention in her final days to return to Strmilov. In 1924, she left Eugene but only made it as far as Iowa City. In such a fragile state, she abandoned her idea. At the end of August, she bought a house at 227 North Dodge Street. In October, she drew up her will. On November 18, 1924, she died at 5:30 p.m. An autopsy attributed her death to cancer. Her body was cremated, and her ashes were placed beneath the Angel with her husband and her son on November 21.

Her estate took years to unravel, for she had promised the people who helped take care of her that she would pay them through her estate. At one point, five lawsuits were set against the estate due to Theresa's unmet promises. Even the city government of Strmilov retained a local attorney, Paul Korab, to represent it in Iowa City. Finally, in March 1931 the estate's net value of $6,893.30 went to the village of Strmilov.

Strangely enough, by some oversight in all the tangled legal wrangling, no money was left to engrave the date of her death on the monument.

ACCIDENT OF OXIDATION: LEGEND, FICTION AND FEAR

By mere accident of oxidation, the Black Angel transformed into the wrong symbol in the wrong place. At its basic iconographic meaning lies contradiction. It is both a symbol of heavenly goodness and purity as an angel and the color of damnation and death by virtue of its blackness. Since medieval times, fallen angels have been rendered as black angels. Death, too, has also been rendered as a dark angel, and among Slavic-speaking cultures, there is a tradition of death personified as a woman. To see it for the first time, a huge, black figure looming over lesser white and gray stones jars our traditional expectations of cemeteries. The juxtaposition demands explanation. Naturally, people are all too happy to supply one, no matter how farfetched.

From 1981 to 1985, Donald F. Johnson, a graduate student studying folklore, collected Black Angel legend stories using interviews and questionnaires from more than one hundred individuals, including teenagers, college-aged students and middle-aged adults. In 1994, Elizabeth Baird used this data in her scholarly paper "Playing with Fear: Interpreting the Adolescent Legend Trip," published in the July 1994 issue of *Western Folklore*. She argues that once local legends are attached to a particular site and become firmly established, the site and the stories are inseparable. The Legend Trip, then, is a pilgrimage to that site to interact—or play— in the context of the legend. In the case of the Black Angel, that means playing with the threat of death.

Most people who have lived in Iowa City have heard about the Black Angel. Many teenagers and young adults who came of age in Iowa City have visited the Black Angel, with a substantial number of them coming at night to dare the unthinkable: touch the statue or kiss under it. Over the years, groups of teens out looking for excitement have gathered at its feet to drink and dare the Angel to live up to its legend. Of course, there are stories that warn of what will happen to those who mess with the statue. Boys who urinate on it are killed later in car wrecks. A boy who strikes it with a sledgehammer loses the use of his arm until he apologizes to the statue. Another boy who saws the thumb from its hand goes insane and is later found strangled in the Chicago River—the sole mark on his throat being a thumbprint. One of Johnson's respondents, a twenty-six-year-old female, said of the spooky stories, "I don't believe them. But under the influence of marijuana, it was more believable."

For Iowa Citians, the Black Angel has come to represent more than just a monument to Theresa Feldwert's love, life and family. Legends have transformed it into a nexus of crisis—where unrelenting death collides with eternal life, where infidelity rejects forgiveness and where deadly vengeance rewards a kiss. A potent and terrifying symbol, the Black Angel has found its way into numerous poems, novels and short stories. William P. Kinsella mentions the Black Angel and Eddie's tomb in his novel *Shoeless Joe Jackson*, which became the hit film *Field of Dreams*. In 1986, he wrote *The Iowa Baseball Confederacy*, in which the Black Angel is a talented right fielder in a two-thousand-inning game against the Chicago Cubs. Children's author Mary Calhoun's *Katie John and Heathcliff* (1980) moved the Black Angel to Missouri for a young girl's first romance. Writers' Workshop alumna and Nebula award nominee Rachel Swirsky featured the Angel in "The Black Angel's Kiss" (2010) as part of her *Through the Drowsy Dark* short fiction and poetry collection. And in 2011, mystery writer Julie Kramer placed the Black Angel as a central device in her novel *Killing Kate*.

Yet even contained safely in fiction, the Black Angel can kick up trouble. *Graveyard Moon* (1995), by Cedar Rapids author Carol Gorman, is a murder mystery for young adults involving a teen's race to reveal a murderer before

Vandalism to the Black Angel's left hand. Some say one trophy taker paid with his life.

she herself is killed. A scene in the book mentions the Black Angel. When a parent considered the Black Angel an affront to her Christian faith, the book was targeted for review by the Cedar Rapids Community School District. In the end, the book was kept on the shelves.

Couples have even been married under the Black Angel. Visitors leave pennies or gifts of flowers at its feet, but notoriety has not been completely kind to the statue. Often, midnight legend trippers climb onto the angel's pedestal, with some even trying to climb onto her back or wings. Four of the fingers on her outstretched left hand, including the thumb, have been cut off, apparently as souvenirs. One can only speculate what fate ultimately rewarded the vandals. Because the cemetery is open to pedestrians around the clock, the Black Angel has its own guardians: the local neighbors, the Iowa City police and the Oakland Cemetery sextons. Even in the twenty-first century, Halloween still requires that the Angel be watched over and protected.

Yet not all odd behavior at the Angel's feet is confined to Halloween. In May 2011, Iowa City police arrested an intoxicated woman who had assaulted her boyfriend. According to the report, the man told officers he and his girlfriend passed out in front of the Black Angel statue in the cemetery. He woke up to her scratching, punching and choking him.

Stranger still—and perhaps more emblematic of Iowa City's preoccupation with the statue—was the June 2010 incident when Iowa City police arrived at the cemetery to arrest an eighteen-year-old man for dancing with the Black Angel. When the man resisted, they tasered him.

Of course, that story has since changed. It now goes that a man once tried to dance with the Black Angel and was struck by lightning.

In Oakland Cemetery, she stands, uncanny and enigmatic. Visit her. Clamber onto the pedestal. Press your fingers into her wounded bronze hands—if you dare. For there are many other stories of ill things that befell those brazen enough to meddle with the Black Angel.

ABOUT THE AUTHOR

Vernon Trollinger grew up in Wyomissing Hills, near the city of Reading, Pennsylvania. He attended the University of Iowa, earning dual BAs in English and theatre arts–communications, and earned his master of arts degree at Iowa from the MAW Expository Writing Program. This promptly led him into a career as a field archaeologist. He has participated in Phase I, II and III Cultural Resource Management projects in Iowa as well as Virginia, including an ossuary excavation in downtown Richmond and the Tredegar Iron Works site (now part of the National Park Service). Returning to Iowa, he co-founded a paranormal-parody 'zine called *Third Eye Over Iowa* with other talented writers in 1996. *Third Eye Over Iowa* ceased publishing in 1999 but maintains a story archive on its website. Vernon now lives a few miles outside Iowa City and works as a freelance copywriter specializing in the energy industry.

Visit us at
www.historypress.net